Ra

Anxious Child

Useful Tips and Helpful Methods for
Supporting Kids with Anxiety from
Childhood to Teenager
2 Books In 1

Katherine Guzman

TABLE OF CONTENT

BOOK 1

Helping Your Anxious Child

"Fight Fears, Overcome Worries, and Cope with Anxiety in Kids"

INTRODUCTION

Finding someone who is absolutely fearless is next to impossible. We all have our fears, worries, and insecurities. It is not just adults; even children harbor all this. Most children are scared of one thing or the other. Some are scared of the dark while others are worried about monsters hiding under the bed. Separation anxiety, excessive fear or worry, panic attacks, social anxiety, and obsessive-compulsive disorder are more common in children than most of us believe. These anxiety-driven conditions can prevent them from leading their life to the fullest and enjoying a happy childhood like they're supposed to.

Unfortunately, the stressful world we live in is becoming increasingly overwhelming for children and adults alike. More and more children these days are incredibly stressed out and exhibiting symptoms of anxiety. Childhood anxiety has become commonplace. Parents and caregivers everywhere worry about what they can do to ease their child's anxiety. Are you wondering what is normal? How can you determine if your child's stress has turned into a severe anxiety disorder? How can you help your child? How can you prevent this anxiety from stressing him out? How can you be a more supportive parent? How do you identify the triggers of anxiety? Are you wondering what causes anxiety? Do you want to help your child break free of this worrying pattern and lead a happy and healthy life? Are all these questions bothering you? If yes, this book is the ideal choice for you. Regardless of how worrying anxiety might seem, it doesn't have to be your child's permanent companion.

There are several things you cannot regulate or control in life. Parenting an anxiety-ridden child might make you feel quite helpless at times. Don't let this worry get the better of you. Even if it seems worrisome, it can be managed. Anxiety can be efficiently managed and overcome. It takes conscious effort, patience, consistency, resilience, and implementation of helpful anxiety-coping techniques. Anxiety can be managed. The first step is to learn more about it. Are you wondering how you can do all this? Well, you no longer have to worry, because *Helping Your Anxious Child: Fight Fears, Overcome Worries and Cope with Anxiety in Kids* has all the information you need. The information given in this book will help reduce and even prevent your child's needless suffering. You can also ensure that he is equipped with all the tools needed to lead a good life tomorrow. As a parent, we all try to create the best possible life for our kids. If you want your child to look forward to a happy and anxietyfree future, this book will come in handy.

In this book, you will learn about understanding fears and anxiety in children, and their common causes and triggers. The first step toward tackling anxiety in your child is to educate yourself about it. Always remember that information is the most powerful tool in your arsenal to tackle anxiety. The more you are aware of anxiety, the easier it is to recognize whether your child is suffering from it or not. You will also be introduced to how anxiety works and the different thought patterns your child might be suffering from. Once you are armed with this information, you will learn to recognize your child's anxiety triggers and his fears or worries. Knowingly or unknowingly, a common mistake most parents (even the well-intentioned ones) make is feeding their child fears. Fear is contagious, and if you are not careful, it can quickly become overwhelming. As a parent, it is your responsibility to stay calm and confident even in stressful circumstances. Remember, your child is depending and counting on you. You need to be his pillar of strength and support during his anxiety.

By understanding the different types of anxiety disorders, the common causes, and how you can help your child cope with them, you can increase his confidence and sense of independence. You should also understand how to stop feeding your child's fears and prevent his fears from feeding his anxiety. When it comes to anxiety, negative thought patterns and behaviors have a direct effect on anxiety. One factor leads to another and it is a vicious cycle. Unless you know what to look for, you cannot help your child overcome anxiety. This is where this book steps into the picture. It will teach you about common myths associated with anxiety, different signs you should watch out for, helping your child understand anxiety, and opening a healthy dialogue about anxiety and mental health. Mental health is as important as physical and emotional health. Even if one of these aspects of your child's life is out of balance, it adversely affects everything else.

Teaching your child to think realistically and providing him with the skills required to face and fight his fears and plan for a brighter future can help him cope with his anxiety. Anxiety is not a condition that goes away overnight. Instead, it takes regular conditioning, healthy changes, and consciously changing thinking and behaviors. It is a lifelong journey. Parenting is a lifelong journey, too, and all the information you need to do all this is given in this book. This book will act as your guide and mentor every step of the way.

Are you wondering how I know all this? Well, I believe a little introduction is needed. My name is Katherine Guzman, and I know what you are experiencing right now. I get how difficult parenting can be at times. It becomes even trickier while dealing with an anxious child. My life is everything I ever hoped for. I have a wonderful husband and a 10-year-old who is the apple of my eye. As a doting mother, I was quite worried when my child started showing symptoms of anxiety. This is when I realized anxiety doesn't just affect adults, but even kids struggle with it. Seeing my little one cling to me at parties instead of mingling with his peers or wake up screaming in the middle of the night used to worry me. My child first started showing signs and symptoms of anxiety about four years ago. I was shocked and alarmed when the pediatrician told me that my son has anxiety!

Instead of getting caught up with all my fears and worries, I decided to embrace this news. Anxiety might sound troubling, but it can be managed. I realized it is not the end of the road. I also realized that my son needed me now more than ever. To deal with his anxiety, I started intensively researching what anxiety means, its causes, common triggers, symptoms, and warning signs, and how to deal with it. I spent countless hours poring over all the books on dealing with anxiety in children. From self-help to psychology and parenting guides, I read everything I could get my hands on. During this journey, I tried different techniques, tips, and strategies to help my child manage and overcome his anxiety. It all started with a simple change in my mindset and attitude about anxiety and mental health. The more I read, the better equipped I was at dealing with it.

I started to see a positive change in how my son dealt with his anxiety. With age, he got better at expressing his emotions, needs, and preferences. We started working as a collective unit to tackle his problem. I began sharing my successful advice with other parents who were in similar situations. This was my aha moment! I realized my personal experiences coupled with all the information I had amassed gave me first-hand experience of how to deal with an anxious child. I decided this information needs to be shared and shouldn't be restricted. Those I shared my tips and suggestions with found it helpful. This was my motivation to write this book. First and foremost, I am a parent concerned about the wellbeing of my child. As a mother, I get how difficult it can be while coping with your little one's anxiety. The good news is, you are not alone.

As you go through the information given in this book, you will understand the different nuances of anxiety and how to deal with it. You will learn about certain dos and don'ts of dealing with your anxious child. You will be introduced to a plethora of techniques that can be effectively taught to your little one to manage his anxiety. You will feel more empowered and confident in your parenting skills and abilities by the end of this book. I will use this book to help parents learn all about anxiety in children, so they can help their children fight their fears, overcome their fears, and cope with their anxiety.

So, are you eager to learn more about all this? If yes, it is the best time to get started.

CHAPTER ONE

Deciphering Childhood Fears And Anxiety

"I am scared of dogs!"

"I don't like meeting new kids."

"Can you check my closet before going to bed?"

"I don't want to be alone at night."

"What if other kids at school don't like me?"

"I can't do this!"

Do these phrases sound familiar to you? If yes, chances are your child is expressing his fears and anxieties through them. The first step to help your child overcome his anxiety is to learn about it.

Diff erence Between Anxiety and Fears

Understanding the diff erence between anxiety and fear is important if you want to help your child. These terms are often used synonymously but are extremely diff erent. They also have overlapping symptoms, and depending on the context, your child's emotional experience will differ. The rudimentary diff erence between fear and anxiety is that fear usually comes from a threat that is known or understood. On the other hand, anxiety comes from a threat that is poorly defi ned or is unknown or unexpected. The stress response triggered by both fear and anxiety is quite similar. For instance, whenever you are scared or anxious, your heart rate increases, your breathing becomes rapid and shallow, and there is muscle tension. All these symptoms are associated with your fi ght-or-fl ight stress response required for survival. Without this essential response, your mind cannot fully perceive and understand the danger signals your body needs to prepare itself to tackle the stressor.

Anxiety is usually described as a feeling of apprehension. It is your response to a threat that is not precisely known or unknown. You might feel this unpleasant response while walking alone on a dark street. It can also be associated with the belief that something bad might happen. If you are walking down an empty street late in the night, the possibility of being harmed can trigger anxiety. It is primarily your mind's interpretation of any possible dangers it senses. Anxiety presents itself with various physical sensations that are incredibly uncomfortable. The most common physical feelings of anxiety are muscle tension, pain, tingling or numbness, hot flashes or cold chills, chest pain, rapid heart rate, shortness of breath, involuntary trembling and shaking, tightness in the body, sleeping difficulties, and digestive troubles.

This brings us to fear. Fear is your body's emotional response when it knows there is a definite threat. Let us go back to the previous example of walking down a dark alley. If an armed assailant startles and points a weapon at you, the danger is present right before you. This danger is not only real, but it is imminent and immediate. This becomes the object of fear in the situation. The focus of the response between fear and anxiety might be different, but it is always interrelated. For instance, anxiety stems from an imagined or perceived danger. Similarly, when scared, we tend to experience all the physical symptoms that were previously discussed.

What Is Normal and When to Worry?

What do the boogeyman in the closet, a spider, and a teacher's rebuke have in common? They are all common fears and anxieties children experience. These are things you don't have to worry much about. It's highly unlikely that your child will agree with you. Fears and worries are common. The only thing that makes a difference is how your child handles them. There are multiple sides to every child's fears. Fears keep us safe to a certain degree. They act as an insurance policy and prevent us from doing things we are not supposed to. Some fears we experience are imbibed into our genetics through evolution. For instance, children and adults continue to fear things that are way outside their experience. Similarly, our brains are hardwired to tell us snakes are dangerous and we should protect ourselves from them. Even though an average individual rarely encounters a venomous snake out in the open, we still believe they are dangerous.

Unfortunately, the trouble starts when these fears and anxieties trigger intense emotional responses to specific events or even things. Some are common while others are worrisome. There are times when you need to worry as a parent and others when you need to let go and believe in your child's development.

For instance, infants and toddlers are scared of separation, changes in the usual environment (such as shifting to a new house), mingling with others, loud noise, sudden movements, and even large objects. During the preschool years, children are usually scared of any noise at night, monsters or ghosts, certain animals such as dogs, and the dark. Some common fears children experience during the school years are injuries and illnesses, doctors, failure, rejection, staying alone at home, natural disasters (such as thunderstorms), snakes, and even spiders. All these fears are not only common but are a rite of passage in childhood. As your child grows, he will slowly overcome these fears. The problem with anxiety is the fear never really goes away and instead, it creates intense emotional feelings and experiences that further worsen the existing fears.

Some degree of anxiety in children is appropriate and not alarming. Your child will have fears that come and go throughout his life. Whenever he encounters a new situation, he will need some time to learn about it. After all, he has just started to learn how the world works and is trying to make sense of it. Once he faces the situation and learns about it, he will get used to it. For instance, a child who has never interacted with a dog might be scared of the animal. After spending some time with a friendly puppy, chances are his fear will change.

As mentioned earlier, anxiety is useful to a certain extent. It helps children and adults alike navigate dangerous situations. For instance, you will feel anxious if you are standing at the edge of a cliff . This natural anxiety and worry keeps us alive. This anxiety is even helpful in social situations. For instance, if someone is being bullied or teased, a child might experience anxiety over such mistreatment. This anxiety can give him the courage required to step up and comfort his friend or even defend him. Unfortunately, society has conditioned us to believe that if a child suff ers from anxiety, it is a refl ection of poor parenting. As discussed previously, children will feel anxious in certain circumstances, and it is perfectly normal.

This brings us to the next question: when is the anxiety a problem that you need to be worried about? There are two red fl ags you need to pay extra attention to when it comes to anxiety, and they're extreme distress and avoidance. Here is a scenario that will give you a better understanding of these red fl ags. Let us assume your child just started school and was incredibly happy during the fi rst couple of days. Later, he started to have meltdowns when he was dropped off at school. In fact, he started crying, throwing tantrums, and gasping for breath on the ride to school. Now, let's consider the situation of a child with sensory processing issues such as autism. If a child is extremely sensitive to loud noises and has a strong dislike for them, any situation where loud noises can be expected will make him extremely anxious and nervous.

In both these scenarios, the child might refuse to go to school, or any other place that triggers his anxiety. Another commonality between these scenarios is the extreme distress they experience. These scenarios are a perfect example of childhood anxiety that parents should be worried about. Anxiety comes in different forms and manifests quite differently. If your child is exhibiting any of the following symptoms, it means his anxiety is not normal.

- He goes to great lengths to avoid specific situations, activities, or people because they make him distressed.
- In any scenario, he constantly worries about everything that can and will go wrong.
- All his fears and worries are effectively interfering with his usual activities and preventing him from performing them.
- Regardless of all the reassurances you give, his distress doesn't go away.
- He struggles to sleep at night or keeps waking up in the middle of the night.
- He also complains about physical symptoms such as stomach pain or headaches that are not due to any other medical conditions.

In all these circumstances, your child is experiencing anxiety. If you notice any of these symptoms, consult your child's healthcare provider immediately.

Chemical Imbalances Results in Anxiety

Different types of chemicals are constantly circulating in your body, such as neurotransmitters, hormones, and enzymes. Increased exposure to stress, lack of sufficient nutrition, injuries, age, and even any illness can create chemical imbalances. Whenever there is any talk about chemical imbalances, it's usually referred to as an imbalance of neurotransmitters in the brain. As the name suggests, neurotransmitters are chemicals responsible for transmitting signals from one neuron (brain cell) to another. They also transmit messages from neurons to muscles and even gland cells.

The pathways of the neural systems at times result in emotional pain such as anxiety due to chemical imbalances. When it comes to anxiety, it's usually a combination of factors that results in this condition. It would be unfair to say genetics are the only factors at play. Even if you have a specific gene that increases your risk of anxiety, it doesn't always have to be the case. If you have a predisposition toward anxiety symptoms, other environmental factors need to be considered as triggers. It's usually an interactive combination of factors at play that triggers anxiety.

The neural pathways and associations are responsible for the neurochemicals transmitting in your body. These neural pathways also determine the strength of the chemicals as they pass through synapses. A synapse is the gap between two neurons in the brain. Your neurochemistry is always determined by neural associations and pathways. Certain hormones are needed to ensure the chemical processes are functioning effectively and efficiently in the brain to maintain your mental and emotional stability. These neurotransmitters help with the production and distribution of serotonin. This hormone is responsible for regulating your mood, cognition, learning, and memory.

A hormonal imbalance reduces the distribution of serotonin, which triggers a chain reaction. The lack of sufficient serotonin increases the risk of anxiety. A primary hormone responsible for anxiety and worry is cortisol. Cortisol is a stress hormone and is a part of your body's fight, flight, or freeze response. This response is embedded into our DNA and is a part of our survival instinct. Usually, as soon as a stressor goes away, the fight-or-flight response goes away, and the cortisol returns to the normal level. When this doesn't happen and there is insufficient serotonin in the body, it increases anxious thoughts and feelings.

CHAPTER TWO

What Causes Anxiety?

Tackling and preventing the manifestation of a problem becomes easier when you are aware of its causes. Anxiety isn't restricted to a single underlying factor. Usually, it is a combination of factors that trigger anxiety and they are as follows.

Genetics Count

If a condition is known as hereditary, it means you either have a high risk of developing it or are born with it. It essentially means the genetic factors or genes were passed onto you through your parents. Genes are a primary part of our DNA. They are present in all the cells in the body. Certain treatments and medicines can also change or activate certain genes. The likelihood of inheriting a disease depends on whether the specific genes are activated or not.

Understanding the link between genetics and anxiety is not a new topic in the scientific community. Decades of research have been directed towards this topic. According to the research undertaken by Deborah J. Morris-Rosendahl (2012), certain chromosomal characteristics are associated with panic disorders and intense fears or phobias. According to the study conducted by Matthew N. Davies et al. (2015), the presence of a specific gene known as RBFOX1 can increase the likelihood of developing a generalized anxiety disorder. In the study, researchers were trying to identify the prevalence of mental illnesses in twins and their genetic makeup. According to another study conducted by Michael G. Gottschalk and Domschke (2016), certain anxiety disorders such as generalized anxiety disorder, panic disorder, and social anxiety disorder are all associated with different genes. Genetic anxiety disorder can be inherited due to its association with different genes, according to a review conducted by Michael G. Gottschalk (2017). From all this research, one thing is certain: genetics play an important role when it comes to anxiety. It's not just environmental factors; even basic biology is at play.

From this research, it is clear that if you have a close relative with anxiety, the risk of developing it is higher. Another conclusion is certain genes increase the risk of developing anxiety. Based on certain environmental triggers, these genes can be turned on or off. Scientists are still trying to understand the specific genes associated with anxiety, and further research is needed until they can come to some conclusion.

If anxiety is hereditary, it doesn't mean everyone in the family will develop it. As mentioned, even environmental factors play a role. If your child faces an extremely stressful situation such as disruption in regular family life or traumatic incident, his risk of developing anxiety increases if he already has the said genes present.

Biological Factors at Play

According to the study conducted by Shao Zheng Qin et al. (2014), certain areas of the brain can also influence the development of anxiety and related problems. The amygdala is known as the brain's fear center. If there are any alterations in the development of this important area of the brain, it increases the risk of developing anxiety-related symptoms. The researchers of the study carefully analyzed 76 children between the age of seven to nine years. It's usually believed that this is the age group during which anxiety-related symptoms and behaviors can first be identified. Parents of these children had to complete various assessments designed for measuring the level of anxiety experienced by the children. These kids also have to undergo a noninvasive MRI (magnetic resonance imaging) scan so the scientist could understand the function and structure of the brain.

During this research, they noticed those with high levels of anxiety had a rather enlarged amygdala. It was not only enlarged, but there was also a rapid increase in the connectivity with other regions of the brain responsible for the perception of emotions, attention, and relation of emotions. These levels were quite high in those with anxiety when compared to those who didn't. Since the amygdala is responsible for fear learning and processing emotions based on information, these alterations in the brain's structure and connectivity resulted in higher levels of anxiety. This study brings research a step closer in the right direction of identifying certain biomarkers associated with an increased risk of anxiety.

Environmental Factors

Apart from the factors mentioned so far, certain environmental factors also play a role in the development of childhood anxiety. Environmental factors refer to the child's usual living environment, relationship with family members or caregivers, and exposure to any traumatic events. Experiencing a traumatic life experience such as dealing with their parents' divorce or even the death of a loved one can be quite overwhelming for a child. It can increase the risk of anxiety.

Similarly, the chance of a child developing anxiety if he doesn't get the required care and support from his primary caregivers is also quite high. If the usual environment at home or school the child is exposed to is incredibly stressful, it increases the risk of anxiety. According to the study conducted by Bethany C. ReebSutherland et al. (2017), environmental factors can increase the risk of anxiety in kids. Though this study was based on animal models, the research suggests exposure to high-quality maternal care early in life reduces the risk of anxiety in offspring.

All these factors are interdependent. Biological factors coupled with genetics and environmental factors significantly increase the risk of developing anxiety and related disorders in kids.

Chapter Three

Understanding the Nuances of Anxiety

Apart from all the diff erent factors discussed in the previous chapter, certain commonly ignored factors are also associated with anxiety. Some children are naturally outgoing while others lean toward introversion . When compared to extroverts, introverts can seem quite anxious. Understanding these nuances gives you a better insight into your child's anxiety.

Personality vs. Anxiety

Your child might be quiet, reserved, or prefer to hang out only with a couple of friends. If so, he is probably shy or introverted. The world we live in is comfortable for extroverts, but what about introverts? An extrovert is quite comfortable in social settings and thrives in such situations. On the other hand, an introvert struggles and can become distressed too. Wrongly labeling your child's introversion or shyness as anxiety can be problematic. The only way to distinguish between these two is by understanding your child's natural personality and not confusing it with anxiety.

When compared to their talkative, outgoing, and slightly impulsive extrovert counterparts, introverts can seem quiet and reserved. They often listen and observe before acting. So how does a child become an introvert? The answer is quite simple actually—they're born that way. Introversion is a part of your child's temperament and a basic characteristic hardwired into him since birth. Introverts and extroverts are built quite differently. A common mistake parents and adults unknowingly make is they wrongly diagnose their child's shyness as social anxiety disorder. There are overlapping similarities, but they are not the same.

Social anxiety disorder is also wrongly understood as an extreme case of shyness. A lot of people fail to get the help needed for social anxiety disorder because they don't recognize it as a psychiatric condition. According to statistics published by the British Psychological Society (2013), even though this disorder shows symptoms and childhood, only half the adults receive the treatment they need. Understand that introverts and shy kids are not just nervous in certain situations. They have a general phobia of social situations. They are quite terrified of how they will be perceived. Even a small interaction such as eating lunch at the school cafeteria can seem like a scary situation for children with social anxiety disorder. This fear is because they worry they might unknowingly do something offensive or embarrassing and others will judge or reject them. Their social anxiety is deep-seated and it transcends the usual meaning of shyness and introversion.

Try to understand your child's personality before wrongly labeling him. Labels tend to stick. For instance, if you brush away your child's social anxiety disorder or separation anxiety and shyness as introversion, you are denying the help he needs. Be an intuitive parent with an inclination toward positive parenting. Talk to your child about his worries. Do not ignore or avoid them. Instead, get to the root of it. By doing this, you get a better insight into what your child is feeling and experiencing.

Role of Developmental Delays

As the name suggests, developmental delay refers to a child who hasn't acquired the developmental skills expected of him at a given age when compared to his peers of the same age. These delays can occur in cognition, motor function, social and behavioral aspects, and language and speech. Different factors cause such delays. Whether it is a genetic or hereditary condition such as Down's syndrome or a metabolic disorder, developmental delays can be quite stressful for the child. Common factors of developmental delays include trauma to the brain, psychosocial trauma (such as post-traumatic stress disorder), infection, prenatal exposure to toxic substances, and disturbances in his usual environment.

A cognitive delay harms your child's ability to think intellectually, manifests as learning difficulties, and also reduces his general awareness. If a child has any cognitive delays, he might have trouble communicating or playing with others. Motor delays occur when your child is unable to coordinate different muscle groups. Whether they are large muscle groups such as the ones present in limbs or smaller ones in hands, these delays can prevent him from performing simple tasks such as holding onto objects or even brushing his teeth.

Another developmental delay is associated with your child's social, emotional, and behavioral aspects. A neurobehavioral disorder such as attention deficit hyperactivity disorder or autism spectrum disorder can harm his social, emotional, and behavioral growth. Due to these imbalances in the brain's development, his ability to process information or react to different situations is quite different from others his age. It can also harm his ability to learn, communicate efficiently with others, or even interact socially. Children with such delays often struggle with their emotional and social skills. Anything from understanding social cues to carrying on a conversation or even initiating conversations become tricky. They might also struggle with handling their emotions or coping with any changes.

Another common delay associated with your child's development is his speech. Speech delay makes it difficult for a child to understand words or even concepts. Having trouble identifying body parts, colors, and shapes to reduced vocabulary and an inability to communicate properly are all symptoms of a speech delay. When compared with other children of his age, he might not be able to form complex sentences or even understand them. Such children usually are quite slow to talk, cannot create meaningful sentences, and mumble.

Are you wondering why you need to understand developmental delays? Once you understand what they are and the areas where your child struggles, it becomes easier to see how it can cause anxiety. For instance, if your child's motor skills are lagging when compared to his peers, he might be worried about it. If all his friends can play ball games but he is still trying to coordinate his muscles, he will feel left out. This can increase the pressure he's already feeling.

According to a review published by David Beck Schatz et al. (2006), a significant portion of children with ADHD and other behavioral delays usually have an anxiety disorder too. The comorbidity between anxiety and ADHD isn't yet fully understood, but research is going on to understand more about it. The potential causes for both these conditions are quite similar and this can be a possible explanation for their comorbidity. According to the research conducted by Valsamma Eapen (2013), developmental delays can increase the risk of mental health disorders, including anxiety disorders in children. If your child is struggling with any developmental disorders, ensure that you address this condition fi rst. It, in turn, will help reduce his anxiety.

Parental Pressure

Parental pressure is quite real. Even well-intended parents tend to unconsciously engage in pressuring their kids to do better. As parents, the child's wellbeing and success become our priorities. Unfortunately, most parents don't realize there is a fi ne line to tread between encouraging and supporting the child and forcing them into things they are not yet ready for. In the previous section, you were introduced to the role of developmental delays and anxiety. If your child is struggling with diff erent types of developmental delays, chances are he's already anxious about it. Now, if you force him when he's not yet ready, you are worsening his anxiety.

All parents have incredible expectations for their children. We are introducing our kids to a world driven by hyper-competition and perfectionism. We are placing increasing importance on performance, appearance, and status. All these things are incredibly stressful for your little one. Even if your idea is to help him succeed, it is merely worsening his mental health. This is considered to be one of the reasons why anxiety, anxiety-related disorders, depression, and other mental health problems are gradually increasing in children.

Societies and their unreasonable standards tend to weigh heavily on children. You might believe you know the best for your child. Well, you are not leading his life. Parental pressure is similar to a hurricane that damages everything in its path. Whether it is the pressure on your child to socialize more, participate in activities, or do things that other kids his age are doing, it is bad for him. Instead of shaping him and equipping him with the skills required to become an independent and confident adult, you are worsening the pressure.

The world we live in is competitive enough. Your child doesn't need more pressure from you. For instance, if your child has social anxiety, he might not be comfortable in social settings. Going to birthday parties might be something most children enjoy, but he might not. Instead of forcing him to attend such parties, acknowledge what he's feeling and help him overcome his anxiety. By forcing him, you are making him more anxious. Instead of being a demanding parent, take responsibility for the pressure you have unknowingly or knowingly caused. When left unregulated, this can become a traumatic experience for your little one.

If your child has obsessive-compulsive disorder or posttraumatic stress disorder, chances are an event has left him traumatized. In the aftermath, your child might not even feel like himself. He is dealing with the mental, emotional, and physical effects of anxiety. As a parent, it is your responsibility to help relieve these side effects before alleviating his anxiety. Once his fear is addressed, he will feel better. It, in turn, will increase his willingness to be more participative in different activities will increase. If your child is worried about riding a bike, don't force or scare him into it. It will worsen the trauma he is experiencing. Instead, show him there's nothing to worry about and work with him to let go of that fear. Once the fear goes away, he will be more than willing to ride the bike!

CHAPTER FOUR

How Does Anxiety Work?

Anxiety disorders occur on a spectrum. Depending on the condition and the severity of the problem, the intensity of your child's anxiety will differ. Some conditions have specific reasons, causes, and triggers, while others don't. Understanding the different types of anxiety disorders helps identify what your child might be possibly suffering from.

Types of Anxiety Disorders

You might have fond memories of your childhood. While growing up, did you always think life is easy? Were there any instances that triggered fear and worries? Well, chances are your child experiences some fears and worries too. Childhood can be quite anxious. Children are not only expected to learn new skills, but they need to face challenges, overcome their fears, and learn to navigate a world that doesn't always make proper sense. At times, all the stress, fears, and worries can become too much for their little bodies and minds to handle. The normal comforts you provide might not serve the purpose anymore. In such instances, the child might develop a diagnosable anxiety disorder.

Fortunately, anxiety can be treated and managed. It doesn't have to be a debilitating condition. Before you learn more about helping your child cope with his anxiety, it is important to understand the diff erent types of anxiety disorders. These disorders are as follows.

Generalized Anxiety

Generalized anxiety is characterized as a disorder when you're worried about a variety of topics ranging from fi nances and natural disasters to relationships and everything else happening in life. There is no specifi c area of your life responsible for your worries because everything becomes worrisome. These worries can be incredibly difficult to regulate and pop up randomly. Focusing on your usual life can become difficult. Children with generalized anxiety disorder usually experience sleep disturbances, muscle tension, reduction in concentration or difficulty paying attention, increased irritability, and fatigue. Your child could probably be worried about family relationships, his friendships, performance at school, and pretty much anything else happening in his life.

Phobias

Any intense fear triggered by a specific situation, object, or animal is known as a phobia. Some common phobias include the fear of injections, going to the dentist, spiders, heights, or dogs. Phobias are often so extreme that an individual with it goes to great extremes to avoid the object or situation that triggers their fears. At times, they experience extreme distress if they try to face it. Fear turns into a phobia when it lasts for at least six months. Learning to distinguish between an age-appropriate fear and phobia is important. For instance, young ones are usually scared of the dark. If a three-year-old is scared of the dark, it doesn't mean she has a phobia. You will learn more about ageappropriate fears and anxieties in the subsequent chapters.

Panic Disorder

It can be quite heart-wrenching when your little one starts crying uncontrollably or is truly inconsolable. A panic disorder is when he experiences panic attacks that prevent him from leading his life. During a panic attack, your child's breathing becomes rapid; he might experience nausea, blurring of vision, shaking, rapid heartbeat, chest pain, and dizziness. He might also be filled with an overwhelming feeling of doom or that the world isn't real. Some complain about an out-of-the-body feeling and experience too.

These attacks can be triggered by something specific or even random occurrences. A panic attack usually reaches its peak intensity within 15 minutes. If a child has this disorder, he probably avoids all situations that can trigger such an attack. He might also experience a constant worry that he will have a similar attack again. It is always better to seek professional help in such situations because a panic disorder shouldn't be confused with a phobia or social anxiety.

Social Anxiety Disorder

If your child has this disorder, chances are he experiences intense fear whenever interacting with his classmates, friends, or even during playtime. This fear manifests itself quite differently. For instance, he might refuse to speak, cling to adults, start crying, or even throw tantrums. Another common symptom of social anxiety disorder is freezing up in social settings. Chances are he will try his best to avoid all social settings and situations that trigger his fears.

Separation Anxiety Disorder

Some form of separation anxiety is quite common in children when they're growing up with this anxiety-related disorder. This is especially true for those between the ages of one to three years. Try to understand that your child is used to your continued presence as a baby and a toddler. If older children start experiencing intense fear or anxiety when separated from their primary caregivers, it can be a sign of separation anxiety disorder. Those with this disorder are commonly plagued with the worry of being separated from their parents and caregivers. This anxiety is so severe your child might start refusing to go anywhere where you are not there. He might also experience physical symptoms such as nausea, headaches, and tummy aches due to this anxiety. Another common symptom you should watch out for is nightmares.

OCD and PTSD

Post-traumatic stress disorder or PTSD and obsessivecompulsive disorder or OCD were previously grouped with other anxiety disorders. Now, they are classified into their own categories. It's not just adults who can experience this, but even children are susceptible to it. These disorders are relatively rare when compared with other forms of anxiety. PTSD is usually triggered due to exposure to a disturbing event. If your child experiences a disturbing event or any series of events that have resulted in unusual coping mechanisms or behaviors, it can be PTSD. If he starts withdrawing himself, has recurring nightmares about the stressful event, has trouble falling asleep, or becomes increasingly clingy and displays other regressive behaviors such as bed-wetting, it can be PTSD.

On the other hand, obsessive-compulsive disorder is the condition wherein children harbor unwanted fears, feelings, and thoughts. These are known as obsessions because they trigger anxiety. To let go of this anxiety they experience, children develop behaviors known as compulsions or rituals. Obsessions are certain fears and thoughts that kids cannot stop thinking about. Your child might be aware of his thoughts but isn't capable of fully making sense of them. For instance, he might believe that breaking a rule or not listening to his parents can have severely harmful consequences, or doing something brings good or bad luck. It essentially results in a condition where he starts performing certain rituals to ensure that everything is in order, safe, clean, or just right. Whether it is washing and cleaning or repeating a specific word or an action, or redoing the same task, there are several ways OCD manifests itself. It is important to seek professional help to get these conditions diagnosed.

Common Myths About Anxiety

Perhaps the most frustrating aspect of parenting a child with anxiety is all the misinformation available these days. The technological revolution has made the availability of information quite easy. After all, all you need to do is enter a query in a search engine and you have all the information needed. Unfortunately, there's a lot of misinformation available about different topics too. Regardless of whom you meet, whether in a personal or professional capacity, everyone seems to have an opinion about anxiety. Seldom are these opinions backed by genuine facts and science. There are several myths about anxiety, and unless you have the right information, you cannot successfully parent an anxious child. In this section, let's bust some common myths about anxiety and replace them with facts.

Myth #1: Anxiety = Poor Parenting

Your parenting style and child's natural personality tend to influence and shape his behavior. That said, anxiety is not the result of poor parenting. From biological predisposition to the general environment, several factors can trigger anxiety. When it comes to dealing with anxiety, it is okay to become aware of your role in raising an anxious child. However, never make the mistake of equating it with poor parenting. You are not the cause of your child's anxiety. Indulging in self-blame will not help you or your child.

Myth #2: Only Adults Suffer From Anxiety Disorders

One of the most common and perhaps damaging myths of all is the assumption that only adults suffer from anxiety disorders. Several reasons can make an adult anxious, such as financial stress, life changes, relationship troubles, or anything else along these lines. Just because adults deal with different worries doesn't mean children are free from worries and stress. Yes, childhood years are relatively easy when compared to the difficulties of adulthood.

According to the research conducted by R. M. Ghandour et al. (2018), approximately 7% of kids between the ages of three and 17 years are diagnosed with anxiety. It means around 4.4 million children in the US alone suffer from clinically diagnosed anxiety and related disorders. These statistics were published by the Center for Disease Control and Prevention (CDC) and it suggests seven to eight out of 100 children suffer from anxiety. These numbers are representative only of the ones who have been clinically diagnosed. Millions of cases go undiagnosed too.

Myth #3: Anxiety Is Synonymous With Laziness

Never assume that anxiety is synonymous with your child's laziness. They are quite brave and hardworking in trying to overcome that anxiety daily. Waking up every day with a mind full of negative thoughts, unpleasant feelings, and difficult emotions is not easy. It takes a lot of courage to prevent these uncomfortable feelings and emotions from taking over. If your child is dealing with anxiety, chances are he withdraws himself and avoids several situations. He's not doing this out of laziness or weakness. If he is unable to do something, chances are it's because of his anxiety. It is a sign that he needs desperate help and support to get over all of it.

Myth #4: The Child Can Stop Feeling Anxious Whenever He Wants To

If only there was a mental switch that helped switch off negative and troubling thoughts. One misconception you need to let go of is that your child can stop feeling anxious whenever he wants to. If only it was that simple, things would be much easier. If your child knew how to stop feeling anxious, don't you think he would have? After all, anxiety prevents him from leading a normal life like his peers. Once anxiety sets in, all rational thought and logic go out the window. Even if your child's fears are unreasonable and his anxiety is caused by an unlikely event such as permanent separation from parents, he cannot understand this! Telling your child that he just needs to relax or calm down doesn't help. Regardless of how logical and sensible your explanations are, it will not get through to him when he's anxious. So, stop believing that your child can instantly turn off his anxiety.

Myth #5: Anxious Children Are Always Shy

Anxiety is not synonymous with personality. Some children are naturally outgoing while others are shy and introverted. Let go of the misconception that anxious children are always shy. Yes, those with social anxiety might struggle in social settings and socializing in general, but this is only one type of anxiety.

Even if a child with social anxiety wants to interact with others, their anxiety prevents them from doing it. On the other hand, shyness is usually a choice that people make because they are more comfortable away from crowds. If your child decides not to interact with others or spend too much time in social settings, it is his choice. It is not anxiety that is preventing him from interacting with others.

Myth #6: Experiencing Something Bad Results in <u>Anxiety</u>

A common misconception about anxiety is that it occurs only if the child experienced something bad. Yes, this can be a probable cause. Specifi c events or incidents that are especially traumatizing can result in anxiety. For instance, a child who has a phobia of spiders might have had a scary encounter with a spider at some point. On the other hand, there are certain types of anxiety disorders that occurred out of the blue. For instance, a child suff ering from separation anxiety might have never been separated from his loved ones but still experiences it.

As mentioned in the earlier chapters, anxiety is triggered by several factors ranging from genetics to the environment. Understanding more about all this increases your ability to deal with an anxious child.

Myth #7: Anxiety is Not a Real Problem

Whether anxiety is diagnosed or not, it is a very real condition. All the different feelings and thoughts associated with anxiety can be paralyzing. They also create negative behavioral cycles and maladaptive coping mechanisms that further worsen the condition. Since anxiety presents itself as varying mental and physical symptoms, it takes a toll on your child's overall health, behavior, and even happiness. Since anything that induces anxiety is difficult to deal with, children often go to great lengths to avoid such triggers. This might seem like misbehavior. If something takes a toll on your child's happiness and health, it is a real problem that cannot be ignored. If he is experiencing anxiety, don't label him as overdramatic or super sensitive. Anxiety is a problem. The sooner you accept, the easier it will be to help your child gain some sense of control.

Never tell your child that whatever he is experiencing is in his head. Even if anxiety is a mental health problem, its physical manifestation cannot be avoided. If your child is anxious, he might experience inexplicable tummy aches, headaches, and fatigue. He will look to you in that situation for comfort and support.

Myth #8: Anxiety Always Looks the Same

We are all unique and how we experience life differs based on our personalities, experiences, and perceptions. Children are unique too, so any anxiety they experience also differs from one child to another. Some children might express their anxiety by shouting, screaming, getting angry, avoiding certain places, or becoming defensive. On the other hand, some might become extremely clingy, hide, or even retreat into their shells. There are several types of anxiety disorders, and how a child experiences them varies greatly. Some children might also experience physical symptoms of anxiety such as rapid breathing, shakes, and tummy troubles. It's not necessary that anxiety presents itself similarly in all children. This is one of the reasons why parents need to be vigilant when it comes to noticing anxiety and symptoms in their kids.

Chapt er Five

What to Do If My Child Has Anxiety?

Now that you are aware of what anxiety means and the diff erent types of anxieties, it is time to determine if your child has anxiety. Don't confuse common childhood fears with an anxiety-related disorder. In this chapter, you will be introduced to diff erent symptoms and manifestations of anxiety to watch out for.

Common Signs of Anxiety

If you are suspicious that your child has anxiety or any other related disorder, you need to be vigilant. It's quite usual for children to feel anxious at times. In the previous sections, you were introduced to different causes of anxiety and the difference between common fears and worry. When it comes to distinguishing between what is normal and what you need to worry about, the line is often blurry. Even if children don't have any anxiety problems, they can display anxious behaviors. For instance, your child may refuse to eat his lunch at school or seem upset for no apparent reason, which would be multiple causes or no cause at all. Anxiety often presents itself as physical, emotional, and behavioral signs and symptoms. Once you go through the information in the section, you will know what to watch out for.

Emotional Signs of Anxiety

- Your child might seem angry or irritable for no apparent reason
- Displays extreme emotional sensitivity
- Frequent crying
- Scared of making even small and common mistakes
- Start worrying about things in the future such as starting high school
- Starts getting uncomfortable or expresses worry when separated from caregivers
- Drop-offs, whether at school, daycare, or even a friend's home, seem scary
- Has recurring nightmares about separation from loved ones
- Constantly worried about losing parents or has nightmares about it

Physical Warning Signs of Anxiety

- Refusal to eat food at school or daycare
- Random stomach aches and headaches for no apparent reason
- Reluctance to use the washroom except the one at home
- Involuntary sweating and shaking under stressful circumstances
- Inexplicably distracted, restless, hyperactive, or fidgety
- Constant tension in muscles and body in general

Difficulty falling or staying asleep Behavioral Manifestations of Anxiety

- Constant questions about "what ifs," especially about disasters and other worrying occurrences
- Refusal to go to school
- Refusal to mingle with others, complete silence, or preoccupation when expected to work in groups
- Lack of willingness to take part in group activities
- Prefers to stay on his own

- Looks for constant approval from adults in his life, such as caregivers, parents, and teachers
- Tantrums and meltdowns for apparently small reasons
- Has an "I can't do it" attitude even without trying

If you have any suspicions that your child has anxiety, all the caregivers and adults in his life need to stay vigilant and look for the abovementioned signs. Talk to your child's teachers, family members, or anyone else who is involved in your child's life. Consciously work to track patterns and notice his behavior. Talk to his teacher if they have noticed any behavioral or learning challenges in your child. Apart from it, ensure that you consult his pediatrician or healthcare provider about the same.

Common Treatment Options for Anxiety

Anxiety is a clinically diagnosable disorder. As with any other health condition, unless it is treated and managed properly, it can manifest as chronic anxiety. Now that you are aware of the common signs to watch out for, its causes, and possible factors at play, it is important that your child gets the professional guidance required. He can learn to manage and overcome his anxiety with little external help. In this section, let's look at some common treatment options available to treat anxiety.

Cognitive-Behavioral Therapy

Cognitive behavioral therapy or CBT is one of the most effi cient ways to treat anxiety disorders. It teaches your child the skills and techniques required to reduce his anxiety on his own. By learning and identifying negative thought patterns and replacing such thoughts and behaviors with positive ones, managing anxiety becomes easier. CBT will also teach him to distinguish realistic thoughts from unrealistic ones. Most of the anxious thoughts are about something that has not yet happened. If your child learns to differentiate between what is happening and what has not yet happened, he can manage his thoughts. Once he learns to control his thoughts, his ability to manage anxiety will automatically improve. In this, your child needs to work with a therapist and consciously and consistently follow whatever he has learned during the therapy sessions. These skills will stay with your child now and forever. Even though it is usually a short-term treatment option, its benefits are long lasting.

Medication

Prescription medicines are commonly used as a part of anxiety treatment. Medication is used as a complementary treatment option with other forms of therapy to manage and overcome anxiety. This can be a short-term or a long-term treatment option depending on the severity of your child's symptoms and his response to the treatment. While consulting your child's healthcare provider, ensure that you follow the policy of full disclosure about any prescription or over-the-counter medicines your child might be using. The doctor will need all the information about your child's health history, family history of illnesses, and other factors before he can prescribe the required medicines.

The most common drugs prescribed to manage anxiety are known as selective serotonin reuptake inhibitors (SSRIs). These are commonly used to treat anxiety disorders in children and adults. Some of these drugs can be used to treat OCD in children too.

Apart from these two commonly used treatment options, two other forms of therapy can be used. The first one is known as acceptance and commitment therapy or ACT and the second is dialectical behavioral therapy or DBT. ACT teaches your child strategies of acceptance and mindfulness. Mindfulness is the simple act of living in the moment and experiencing everything that happens without any judgment. It teaches him to stay in the moment instead of getting worried about what might happen. Since anxiety often stems from the fear of the unknown, by teaching him to stay in the moment, you reduce the risk of anxiety. Mindfulness and acceptance equip your child with the skills required to manage any unwanted or unpleasant feelings, thoughts, and sensations. Dialectical behavioral therapy is designed to help your child accept responsibility for his problems. By showing him how to deal with conflict instead of transforming them into intense negative emotions, his ability to deal with anxiety will improve.

All children are unique and there is no hard and fast rule that what works for one will work for everyone. Some children might respond better to a specific treatment while others need something else. Apart from these common treatment options, there are certain tips and tactics you can follow, and small changes that you can make to your parenting style that will help your child learn to manage his anxiety. You will learn more about all these in the subsequent chapters.

CHAPTER SIX

Learn And Teach About Anxiety

An important aspect of helping your child tackle anxiety is to talk to him about it. Before you can talk to your child about anxiety, ensure that you have all the information you need. This is a conversation that requires a little preparation. In this chapter, you will learn simple techniques you can use while talking about anxiety. You will also learn about some common mistakes to be avoided while having this discussion.

Talk to Your Child About Anxiety

The importance of mental health is being recognized and accepted slowly by society. Until a couple of years ago, conversations about mental health problems and how to deal with them were taboo. Fortunately, these notions are slowly changing. That said, it is saddening that children and teens often don't understand that they're experiencing anxiety. They might even not recognize the anxiety for what it truly is. Instead, chances are they start believing something is wrong with them. For instance, it's quite easy to fixate on the physical manifestations of anxiety, such as stomach aches or unpredictable mood swings. It wouldn't be surprising if your child starts believing he is weak or going out of control due to anxiety. The problem with these thoughts is they're not only debilitating, they also worsen the anxiety and self-consciousness your child is already experiencing.

As a parent, it is important to start talking to a child about what anxiety feels like. Unless you open a healthy and honest conversation about this topic, don't expect your child to be forthcoming. If you have any preexisting notions that talking about anxiety will worsen his anxiety, time to change this. Usually, fears or problems are worse in our heads than they really are. This is true for not just adults, even kids too. So, stop shying away from the topic of mental health and make it a part of daily conversations. If you talk to your child about anxiety and offer helpful information, it becomes easier for him to understand what he's experiencing, its causes or potential reasons, and what can be done to manage it. In this section, let's look at simple steps to follow while talking about anxiety.

Talking About Fears and Worries

In the earlier chapter, you were introduced to the concept of fears and worries, and the common causes of anxiety. Most anxious thoughts stem from known or unknown fears and worries embedded deep in our psyche. The simplest way to start talking about anxiety is by sharing your worries and fears. Perhaps you can sit with your little one and talk about something you were scared of in your childhood. You can talk about how self-conscious you used to feel while meeting people for the first time. Look for fears or worries that you harbored when you were the same age as your kid. Once you talk about these fears and worries, ask him if he has any of these similar worries of yours.

Another simple way to start a conversation about anxiety is by describing a recent situation where you noticed some signs of anxiety displayed by your child. Perhaps he seemed anxious while visiting a new place, had visitors over to your house, or it was a school-related situation. If you notice that your child is anxious, it is important to talk about it and not brush the topic away. Mental health is as important as your child's physical well being. Ignoring, avoiding, or brushing away these instances can prove detrimental to his overall wellbeing and growth. For instance, if you notice that your child was quiet when you had a visitor over, ask him if he was nervous about having a visitor over. Whenever you talk to your little one about this topic, don't use an accusatory tone. There should be no accusations, blaming, or anything negative associated with this conversation.

If your child starts opening up about his anxieties or worries, offer all the reassurance he needs. Tell him it is okay to have these feelings. Remember, his cues of dealing with his worries and fears will depend on how you deal with them. If he sees you panic, he will panic too. Whatever you do, don't lose your cool and instead, showcase your acceptance of his thoughts.

While doing this, don't tell your child to simply relax or stop worrying. It's quite similar to telling a depressed person to stop being sad and become happy. This is not how mental health works. There is no switch that can be turned on or off. If your child is anxious about something and he constantly hears, "don't worry, it'll be okay," "there is no problem here," or "can you stop worrying?" it will worsen the situation. Showing a little empathy can work wonders at the stage.

Delving Into the World of Anxiety

Now that your child has accepted or has started talking about his worries and fears, it is time to communicate what anxiety means. Before you can talk to him about all this, ensure that you spend sufficient time reading through all the information given in the previous chapters. If you feel it's necessary, consult a professional and prepare yourself for this session. You are talking to an impressionable young adult and you need to have the right information.

"Anxiety is not dangerous." Your child might feel uncomfortable whenever he is anxious. Fortunately, this uncomfortable feeling is not permanent. Since you understand this, talk to your child about the same. Tell him that anxiety is not a dangerous or a life-threatening condition. It is not a problem that needs to be worried about as long as you learn to control it.

"Anxiety is quite normal." The simplest way to make your child feel comfortable talking about anxiety is by stating that it is quite normal. Children are already experiencing a lot of changes in their lives while growing up. If they start feeling abnormal because they are experiencing things others are not, it nearly worsens their stress. If you want your child to get over his anxiety, tell him it is perfectly normal. For instance, you can feel anxious right before an exam or while riding a roller coaster. Depending on your child's approach to problem solving, offer required information. If you believe your kid feels better when he has helpful information and facts, offer the same.

"Anxiety is a natural defense mechanism." An efficient way to normalize anxiety is by explaining how it works. Anxiety is a part of our body's natural defense and adaptive mechanism. Tell your kid that whether it is a wild animal chasing him down the forest floor or while preparing for an important test, we all experience anxiety. Anxiety essentially triggers our fight, flight, or freeze response. As the name suggests, your body starts preparing itself for fleeing the threat, fighting it, or freezing.

If he's still struggling to understand this, ask him how he feels before a very important test, big game, or even a speech. Help him identify how his heart beats faster and the body prepares to fight the danger, run away from it, or wait for it to pass. This response is known as anxious arousal. Tell him that as a species, this natural mechanism is a vital part of our survival process. Whenever we experience any anxiety, we fight, flee, or freeze. Perhaps your child has tried to avoid a situation that makes him anxious by escaping it, or maybe he is used to getting angry and lashing out. Another possible response is he completely freezes, his mind goes blank, and he cannot really think. Ask him if he has ever experienced any of these situations. If he has, it will give him a better sense of what anxiety means and how it works.

"Anxiety is like a smoke alarm." Anxiety becomes problematic when it presents itself despite the absence of danger or threat. If your body is constantly in a state of anxious arousal, it cannot function effectively or optimally. In the previous sections, you were asked to normalize childhood anxiety. Yes, worrying and fears are normal, but these are thoughts that need to be regulated. If your child starts living his life based on these fears and worries, he will never get anything done.

Now, it is time to talk to your child about how anxiety can become problematic. A simple analogy is a smoke alarm response. How does the smoke alarm work? A smoke alarm goes off in case of a fire. If the smoke alarm is too sensitive, it might go off even when there is no fire. For instance, the smoke alarm might start ringing if the toast is burning or the cake you are trying hard to bake has turned to ash. Neither of these situations is life-threatening. Unfortunately, the smoke alarm doesn't understand all of this. By using this analogy, an anxious child's internal smoke alarm is malfunctioning and triggering anxiety despite no obvious smoke. The real problem is one neither of these things works like they are supposed to.

Identifying Anxiety

It is important to help your child recognize his anxiety. Perhaps you can tell him that you will be playing the role of detectives and start an investigation about understanding anxiety. There are three steps you need to follow. The first step is to recognize physical symptoms, the second is recognizing anxious thoughts, and the third is recognizing avoidance. Let us look in detail at all these steps.

It's time to recognize the physical symptoms of anxiety. Perhaps you can start with an outline of the human body and ask your kid to identify where he experiences anxiety. For instance, you can tell him that you experience butterfl ies in your stomach whenever you are doing something new. Or maybe you experience a lump in your throat before a big presentation at work. Depending on your child's age, you can either ask him to point this out on his body or talk about it.

Depending on your child's age, you need to identify his anxiety. For instance, with a young child, you could ask him to give his anxiety a specifi c name such as the Worry Monster, Mr. Always Worried, or Ms. Worry. On the other hand, older kids might be better responsive to a music analogy. For instance, anxiety is similar to the volume being turned up until it hits an uncomfortable level. Talking about identifying the physical symptoms of anxiety is important to manage it. If your child is aware of the physical cues it comes with, he can take corrective action before anxiety is triggered.

The next step is to help your child identify anxious thoughts. Identifying such thoughts is seldom pleasant and even adults struggle with it. This might not be an easy process, but you need to help your child identify negative or dangerous self-talk which is resulting in his anxiety. For instance, ask your child what he thinks while trying something new. Ask him what he felt on the first day of school. Give him an example of a situation and make note of his reaction. You can ask him how he would feel if he thinks that the first of a school would be quite easy and pleasant. Similarly, ask him how his first day would be if he thinks that others would not like him.

The final step of this process is to recognize avoidance. Here are some questions you can ask your child.

- If you woke up one morning and realized your anxiety disappeared, what would you do?
- What is the first thing you would do and how would you react?
- Is there any specific way in which your friends, family, or teachers would know that you were not anxious anymore?

After your child has given these answers, encourage him to finish the next two sentences.

- My anxiety is preventing me from...
- When I'm not anxious, I can finally...

After your child has completed these three steps, he will have a better understanding of anxiety.

You will also be better equipped to recognize anxiety and deal with any avoidance.

What Not To Do

Parenting is not an easy job and it becomes even more difficult when dealing with a child with an anxiety disorder. The first thing you need to do is normalize anxiety and not make a big deal of it. Try to understand that anxious children are dealing with their worries and need you for support and comfort. Even a well-meaning parent might utter words that, instead of alleviating feelings of anxiety, may worsen it. Since you are not experiencing your child's anxiety, chances are that unknowingly, you might make statements that dismiss his feelings. As adults, we don't enjoy being dismissed or told our feelings are not important or don't matter.

Yes, it can be incredibly difficult to watch your child struggle with anxiety. As a parent, your only role in this process is to help him manage and cope with his feelings while removing any potential triggers. In such situations, you need to stay calm, quiet, and positive. The temptation of trying to fix the anxiety can be quite high. Avoid giving in to the temptation because your child takes his behavioral cues from you. Your response to his anxiety can create maladaptive coping mechanisms.

Here are 10 things you should never say while dealing with an anxious child.

It's Not A Big Deal

Perspectives can be quite deceiving in life. Unless you are experiencing something, you don't understand the true intensity or gravity of the situation. This is one of the reasons why most of us struggle with empathy. Unless we have lived through a situation, we don't know what the other person is experiencing. For an anxious child, his worries are a big deal. These worries prevent him from leading a healthy and happy life. They stop him from interacting with his peers and building lasting relationships; they affect his family relationships and can also reduce his performance at school. All these things are a major part of a child's life. These things are a big deal. Instead of telling your child his anxiety is not a big deal, talk about it. Tell him that you understand he's anxious about something. Perhaps you can try a deep breathing exercise or a calming activity.

Stop Worrying

Regardless of how hard you try, you cannot eliminate your child's anxiety by merely telling him "don't worry" or "stop worrying." If only it was this easy. Understand that your child is already worrying. By making such a statement, you are essentially conveying the message that his worries are unacceptable and unreasonable. Apart from invalidating his worries, you make it seem that what he's feeling is not acceptable. This can further intensify and worsen his anxiety. Instead of a dismissive comment, you could probably ask him, "Why don't you tell me more about what you are feeling?" or "Can you tell me about what is worrying you right now?"

There's Nothing To Be Scared Of

We are all scared of different things in our lives. Whether it is judgment or rejection by our peers, these fears never go away. Most of us are scared of failing. The list of fears is truly endless. Understand that your anxious child is also experiencing all these fears. A quick kiss or a pat on the back doesn't dismiss his anxiety or relieve it. If your child is scared of something, telling him that he shouldn't be scared does not work. The best thing you can do is help ease his fears by starting a healthy and positive conversation about it. Fears lose their power when the person dealing with them starts talking about them. This advice applies to children too. Instead of telling him there is nothing to be afraid of, tell your child that you are there with him and you can both fight the fears together. Tell him it is important to talk about his fears instead of keeping them to himself.

You'll Be Fine

Do you ever feel fine when you're overwhelmed by stress and worries? Fine is probably the last thing you feel in such instances. Now, imagine how your child feels if you tell him that he's fine or that he will be fine while dealing with anxiety. This is not an emotion that usually resonates with an anxious mind. His mind is racing and he is overwrought with worries and feelings he is not fully equipped to deal with; he will not feel anything even remotely resembling fine. Instead of telling him that he's fine or he'll be fine, show you are there for him. It's not just your actions, even the words matter. By telling him that you are there for him and he can depend on you, it will ease anxiety.

I'll Do It For You

All children crave independence. An anxious child is no different. Unfortunately, his anxiety usually gets in the way of his need for independence and the strength required to confront his worries. As a parent, you might feel quite helpless to see your child suffer on his own. You might be tempted to swoop in and fix it for him. If you constantly do things for him, try to fix what he's feeling, or don't let him feel what he wants to, it doesn't teach him healthy coping skills. Instead, it teaches him to become codependent. As a parent, it's your responsibility to equip your child with the required life skills and coping mechanisms to get through his life independently. If your child is struggling with anxiety, here is a simple positive phrase you can use. Tell him, "I know how you are feeling right now, and I get it. But I also know you can get through this. I will always be here to support you." At times, all it takes is a little positive encouragement to keep going.

You Need More Sleep

Have you ever struggled to sleep at night while your mind is racing at 100 miles per hour? Maybe you were anxious about a presentation or an interview at work. Whatever the reason, chances are you've experienced anxious nights. If you have ever felt like this, imagine what your child must be feeling! One of the most difficult parts of dealing with childhood anxiety is the inability to go to sleep at night. A worried mind struggles to slow down at the end of the day and rest. Put yourself in your child's shoes and try to perceive the situation from his view. He is not doing this voluntarily and it is not his fault. He needs you to help him sleep some more. So, if you tell him all he needs some more sleep, you're not being helpful. It's merely counterproductive. Instead, here is another approach you can try. Why don't you tell him that you both can spend some time and use a meditation app before bed to promote overall relaxation and better sleep at night?

Stop Thinking

Anyone who has experienced anxiety would love to break free of it. Anxiety is never pleasant and all it does is worsen and amplify all sorts of negative emotions. Well, your child would love to stop feeling anxious right away. It might sound quite easy because anxiety is thought-based. Unfortunately, regulating your thoughts is not an easy process. Even adults struggle with it. How can you expect your little one to understand how to stop anxious thoughts? A positive way to deal with his anxiety is by encouraging him to talk about his anxious thoughts. Start a conversation about what he's feeling, its reasons, and what he wants to do about it. By making him more engaged in this process, you are easing his anxiety.

Can You Hurry Up?

Anxiety can be debilitating. Regardless of what you choose to believe, when your mind is overwhelmed, you cannot process thoughts effectively or efficiently. Understand your child is feeling the same right now. When it comes to parenting, you need to let go of all notions of perfection. Perfectionism is nothing more than a mirage you are chasing. All it leads to is disappointment and negativity. Avoid getting caught in this trap. Anxious kids can be quite slow and usually move at a snail's pace due to their overwhelmed brains. If you ask him to hurry up or force him into things he is not yet ready to do, it merely increases his guilt. If your child already sees his peers do things he's struggling too, such as interact freely with strangers or make friends, telling him to hurry up increases his guilt. If you don't want your child to feel helpless or guilty, stop telling him to hurry up. Instead, ask him what you could do to help.

It's In Your Head

Yes, anxiety is a mood and brain-related disorder. If you dismiss it and tell him it's all in his head, you are merely shaming him. Instead of helping him tackle the anxiety is experiencing, you are increasing his guilt. A simple phrase you should refrain from uttering is, "It's all in your head." Instead, try a more constructive approach. If you realize your child is anxious, tell him his brain is worrying loud right now. Why don't you both practice a relaxing activity to help calm his brain and reduce worries? Perhaps you can go for a walk or visit the nearby park!

I Don't Understand What You Need

One of the worst things you can tell an already anxious child is that you have no idea what he needs. Parenting an anxious child is seldom easy and it can be incredibly exhausting at times. Regardless of what you do, always keep your calm. Remember, your child is depending on you to stay calm and strong to cope with his anxiety. If you express hopelessness, your child will feel worse. It will also heighten his anxiety. Instead of telling him you have no idea what he needs or what has to be done, it's always better to ask him for suggestions. Why don't you ask your child what he would want you to do or what he needs in a given moment? These simple questions help start a positive conversation about anxiety without any unnecessary judgment or shame.

Coping with anxiety takes plenty of time, effort, and consistency. Your child might not have any intention of asking the same question repeatedly or cling to you in social settings. He might also not want to fall apart at the mall or the grocery store. You might think dealing with an anxious child is difficult. Remember, it is always worse for your child. He's still coming to a grip with all the developments going on in his life. Anxiety is just an ordered form of stress. Apart from seeking professional help, the best you can do is be empathetic and compassionate when your child talks about his worries.

CHAPTER SEAVEN

Helping Kids with Anxiety

Acommon response that parents and primary caregivers have in the life of an anxious child is to step in to solve all their problems. If your kid has any anxious thoughts and feelings, you will want to step in and get rid of these thoughts and feelings. If possible, you will also try to eliminate all sources of such anxiety. For instance, if your child is extremely scared of dogs, it's a reasonable assumption that you would want to keep him away from the neighbor's dog. You might think you are helping, but all of this is counterproductive.

When you help your child avoid all scary situations, you are fueling his anxiety. Instead of equipping him with the required skills to manage anxiety, you are encouraging him to harbor more fears. Apart from this, you are also depriving him of opportunities to learn important coping skills to manage his anxiety. In this section, let's look at some simple tips you can follow to support your anxious child.

Tips for Dealing With Separation Anxiety

Separation anxiety is quite common in infants, toddlers, and even preschoolers. So by the time your child is three years old, he fully understands the anxiety associated with separation. By now, he also understands the effect of this anxiety on his life. Parents and children alike need to prepare themselves and create a plan of action to tackle separation anxiety. In this section, let's look at some simple tips you can use to help your child manage his separation anxiety.

A Goodbye Ritual

Create a quick goodbye ritual that can be used whenever you need to say bye to your child. Whether you were dropping him off at school, the local park, or even his grandma's house, a quick goodbye ritual helps. Always keep the goodbye ritual short, simple, and sweet. Never leave with any fanfare. The longer you linger, the more difficult the transition gets. Ensure that you consistently practice this goodbye ritual whenever you are separating from your child. In a way, it slowly conditions his mind to get used to the separation.

Always Keep Your Promises

It becomes easier for the child to make it through the separation if you keep your promises. If you tell him you will be back to pick him up at a certain time, ensure that you keep this promise. Never make a promise you cannot keep. Regardless of whether he has separation anxiety or not, don't break your promises. It not only teaches him that promises can be broken, but it can create mistrust too.

Undivided Love and Attention

Children not only love their parents' undivided loving attention but also thrive in it. Whenever you need to separate from your child, ensure that you give him your undivided love and attention for a couple of minutes before saying goodbye. Once you have said goodbye, ensure that you quickly dismiss yourself from the situation regardless of all his cries and pleads for you to stay. At times, dealing with separation anxiety in a child is similar to Ferberizing a baby to sleep.

Learn to Be Specific

Separation anxiety stems from an unknown fear of being permanently separated from parents or caregivers. It can manifest as a fear of parents or caregivers falling ill or dying. Since a child is gripped with crippling worries, it's important to talk to him about it. Whenever you leave your child or drop him off somewhere, reassure him that you will be back at a specific time. For instance, if you are dropping off your child at school, mention that you will be back in the evening to pick him up when school ends. Similarly, if you are going somewhere for a conference, tell him when you will be back. While talking to your little one about time, ensure that he understands what you are saying. For instance, if your child is too young and doesn't understand what 3:00 PM means, you can tell him, "Mommy will be back by the time you wake up from your nap and want to eat a snack."

Practice Some Distance

A simple way to get your child accustomed to being away from you is by creating some distance. Whether it is a sleepover at his grandma or friend's home, do this. Initially, your child might refuse to spend the night away from you. In such an instance, encourage him to spend an hour away. Slowly increase this time to two hours, and so on until he can stay for prolonged periods away from you. The simple technique gives your child a chance to prepare himself for separation without letting the anxiety get the better of him.

As your child grows and you practice these steps, the chances of his separation anxiety occurring will reduce. He will learn to adapt without you. Consulting your child pediatrician might offer help and insight into this problem.

Tips for Dealing With Social Anxiety

Children with social anxiety are scared of making mistakes and have an intense fear of failure. It also prevents them from experimenting and trying new things. Your child might not truly understand his potential or even discover his likes if he doesn't get out of his comfort zone. Social anxiety prevents him from doing this. In this section, let's look at some tips you can use to help your child deal with it.

Engage with and help your child by using the PACE technique. It stands for playfulness, acceptance, curiosity, and empathy. This helps your child let go of some of the anxiety he experiences in a situation. Instead of being serious all the time, try a playful approach while dealing with anxiety. If you are calm and composed, your child will automatically pick on your energy and feel it too. Start accepting your child's feelings and communicate the same to him. This will reduce his worries and ease the fear of being judged. When he knows he will be accepted regardless of whatever happens, he will feel more confident to tackle the situation. Be curious and ask him what he's feeling during a stressful situation.

Apart from this, show some empathy. This technique helps you connect with your child.

You must talk to him about social anxiety and what it means. You can use this opportunity to discuss some symptoms of anxiety and teach him self-soothing mechanisms. You will learn more about these techniques in the subsequent chapters. A simple way to start a conversation about social anxiety is by admitting that even you get nervous. Encourage the child to admit when he's nervous about something, and to take the first step despite his nervousness. Ask for his feedback after he has performed the activity he was nervous about.

If you believe any activity or scenario in the future will trigger his anxiety, prepare him for it. When a child has all the information about what to expect, managing his anxiety becomes easier. Instead of springing a random event on him that might trigger his anxiety, talking to him about it is always a better option. Discuss in great detail what will happen, when it will happen, how many people will be there, how he needs to respond, and what he will be doing in the given situation. The more information he has, the lesser is the scope for anxious thoughts creeping in. Anxiety is often triggered by missing pieces of information. By talking about it, you reduce the risk of this happening.

Help your child overcome his social anxiety by concentrating more on the process instead of the progress he makes. Taking part in the process is important. If your child is scared of meeting new people, spending time in public settings, or doing anything because he's worried about being judged, encourage him to do all of this. It doesn't matter whether he succeeds or not. The only thing that matters is he took the first step and made some progress. Whenever he makes some progress, offer positive reinforcement. Never expect perfection in life. Expecting perfection from your child is nothing more than a recipe for disaster for everyone involved. It will also increase the stress he feels in a given situation.

An anxious child's anxiety worsens when a parent constantly hovers around them. Don't be a hovering or a helicopter parent. Instead, take a step back. Learn when you need to stop and when to cut your child some slack. Don't try to swoop in and save the day as soon as you notice any mild distress. Wait until he asks for help. Encourage him to solve his problems before you try to save the day.

Schedule some worry time for your child and teach him coping mechanisms. Some common anxiety-coping mechanisms are deep breathing, progressive relaxation, listening to music, and so on. You will learn more about these topics in the subsequent chapters.

Tips for Dealing With Panic Disorder

Panic attacks occur unexpectedly and they are severe episodes of anxiety. These seemingly random out-of-the-blue attacks without any obvious triggers can be quite frightening for the child. As a parent, you might be quite worried when you see your little one struggling with a panic attack. You can also feel a little helpless because of her. You can help him regulate his anxiety by following the different tips discussed in this section to deal with panic disorder.

Always Stay in Control

Your child will lose complete control of himself during a panic attack. So, it is important that you stay completely in control during this attack. Keep calm, talk to him in a gentle and soothing tone, and reassure him. He'll need time and space to calm down and you need to stay in control of the situation.

Talk About Panic Attacks

Your child might be worried about different things associated with a panic attack. It is quite frightening for him to deal with all of it. From the symptoms to unpleasant thoughts and emotions it triggers, it can be too much to handle. He is probably worried that others might ridicule him. He might be scared of losing complete control of his body and mind during the attack itself. The simplest thing you can do to reduce these worries is to talk more about panic attacks. Explain what panic attacks are, how they occur, and what his body feels like during such an attack. Tell him that these panic attacks are quite common and he shouldn't worry too much about them. Another simple way to dispel his worries is to tell him panic attacks are not forever and they are brief. He needs to know that it is okay for him to panic without worrying about judgment from others.

Practice Breathing Exercises

Now that your child understands what a panic attack is and that there is no shame in experiencing it, the next step is to help him gain some sense of control. The simplest way to do this is by practicing breathing exercises. Breathing exercises help calm his body and mind when he's panicking. A panic attack can make him feel quite busy, light-headed, and induce chest pains too. By regulating his breathing, these physical symptoms will go away. Once the physical symptoms go away and his body is calm, the panic attack will ease. Ask him to close his eyes during a panic attack, and take a deep and slow breath through his nose. Encourage him to hold his breath for a second or two before slowly exhaling through his mouth. Breathing through the nose and exhaling through the mouth reduces the physical symptoms of this attack. You can also teach him some selfsoothing techniques discussed in the subsequent chapters.

Overcome Fears

If your child's panic attacks are due to specific objects or situations, facing his fears can reduce the risk of these attacks. For instance, if staying in a closed space is a trigger, gradually expose him to this fear. This means he might be scared of traveling in the car or even sitting in his room. Encourage him to slowly spend more time in the car. Come up with fun games and activities you both can play to ease his worries. Fears are often irrational and encouraging him to face them takes away their power over him. You will learn more about helping your child face and manage his fears in the subsequent chapters.

Shift Your Child's Focus

Your child will have several negative thoughts during a panic attack. By shifting his focus to something else like more encouraging, positive, or happier thoughts, the panic he feels will slowly go away. Whether it is his favorite toy or photograph of happy memory, shifting his brain's focus is important. By asking him to go to his happy place or thinking of a happier time, he can calm his mind.

Challenge the Negative Thoughts

How your child thinks influences the severity of the panic he experiences. If most of his thoughts are beyond his control and are negative, it will be unhelpful. By helping him realize his thoughts are not true or are not supported by facts, these unhelpful thoughts can be changed into something more positive or even realistic. You will learn more about teaching realistic thinking to your child in subsequent chapters. For instance, during a panic attack, he might believe he is having a heart attack, which worsens his panic. By helping him challenge this thought and reminding him that it's not a heart attack, the reality of any panic he feels will reduce.

Keep Reassuring Your Child

Apart from all the different tips discussed in the section, there is another thing you need to do and that is to keep reassuring your child during panic attacks. Tell him this too shall pass and it is not a permanent fixture in his life. Even if it feels as if the panic will never ease, tell him it will go away. This is why you need to stay calm and composed when your child is panicking. Reassure that you are there with him every step of the way and he is not alone.

Tips to Deal With Obsessive-Compulsive Disorder

(OCD)

When your child feels distressed, you will want to make him feel better. Unknowingly, you might be reinforcing your child's OCD symptoms by performing a routine he demands, changing your behavior to accommodate his rituals, or offering more reassurance than required. When you do all these things, you are unintentionally reinforcing his OCD. Another unintended consequence of such acts is it teaches your child that it is okay to engage in obsessive or compulsive rituals and thoughts. Here are all the different types you can follow to help your child deal with his OCD.

Start By Setting Limits

Seeing your child in distress is not easy. The failure to set any limits can make it even harder for him to recover from OCD. For instance, if your child insists that you cannot enter his room without washing your hands, don't encourage this behavior. An ideal response is to talk to him about his OCD and tell him that you understand how difficult it is for him. After this, set a firm limit that you will not be washing your hands every time you need to enter his room. He might have an outburst or meltdown when you set these limits. You should expect them initially. After a while, he will also get used to this consistency and his anxiety will reduce. By establishing certain boundaries and following them consistently, you are discouraging his obsessive or compulsive behavior and rituals.

Learn To Be Firm

This tip is in tandem with the previous one. It's not just about setting limits, you need to be quite firm with your child. You need to put your foot down and tell him that you will not be encouraging his OCD. If you set a rule, follow through and set consequences for breaking it. That said, don't hurt or punish him whenever he breaks the rules. For instance, if your child believes he needs to lock the door five times to make sure it is firmly locked, tell him you will be doing it only once. Tell him the door is locked and stick by this. Don't encourage him.

Don't Accommodate OCD

Don't try to accommodate his obsessive or compulsive behaviors and rituals. Accommodating them essentially means you are taking part in his ritual by changing your behaviors. When you do this, it motivates him to stick to his rituals instead of working on changing them. Simple acts of accommodation include excessive reassurance; changing your lifestyle, behavior, and plans because of his OCD; or following his compulsive rituals. For instance, if your child is scared of germs and believes he cannot touch anything until it is cleaned thrice, don't do this. When you start accommodating his compulsions or isolated symptoms of OCD, you are enabling his disorder. Don't strengthen or prolong this disorder and try to avoid it. Do not enable his rational thoughts, and instead, work on discrediting them.

Some Don'ts

Don't try to use logic or reason. It might seem like a rational thing to do. After all, your child's OCD behavior and rituals are not logical. However, understand that you are not trying to reason with your child, but with the OCD in his brain. Similarly, do not offer any reassurance to him and tell him not to worry. Don't tell him everyone is safe and okay or that bad things will not happen. You might temporarily ease his discomfort, but it does not offer long-lasting relief. Unless your child learns to stand up for himself, his OCD will keep recurring. Instead, when he is calm, talk to him about his compulsions and obsessions. Reason with him, and present logic only when he is calm and willing to listen.

Don't tell him to stop his behaviors. This is not something your child invented. OCD is similar to a constant and incessant whispering in his head that tells him to do something. There are a lot of negative thoughts also associated with OCD. So, telling your child to stop his behaviors is not an effective treatment. Do not blame him because he is the victim of this disorder. At the same time, don't punish him for giving in to his compulsions. Instead, explain that all the scary thoughts that he has about doing something specific are because of his OCD. Educating him is a great way to reduce the power of all those bizarre and scary thoughts in his mind. Encourage him to separate himself from his OCD.

Be Encouraging

Encourage your child to slowly postpone and change his rituals. Keep doing this until he stops performing the rituals altogether. You can do this by asking what would happen if he doesn't do something. For instance, if your child believes something bad will happen if he doesn't wash his hands five times, encourage him to wash his hands only thrice. Ask him if something bad happened. When nothing bad happens, ask him to wash his hand only twice. Do this until you are down to washing his hands only once. By encouraging him to break free of his patterns and realizing that nothing bad is going to happen because of it, you are slowly replacing the irrational thought with something realistic.

Consistent Approach

Once you have devised a plan to tackle your child's OCD, ensure all adults and caregivers in his life follow this plan too. There needs to be consistency in practice. Consistency brings a sense of comforting familiarity your child will appreciate. The lack of consistency merely increases confusion and will leave your child bewildered. For instance, if other members in the household accommodate his behaviors while you curtail them, he will not know what's expected of him. It will worsen any stress he experiences and his OCD might worsen. For instance, if your idea is to reduce your child's repetitive behaviors, a simple rule you can use is to repeat the behavior only twice. Once you have said this rule, ensure that all the caregivers in his life follow through. While you do this, you need to talk about the decision and the agreed-upon consequences. If one caregiver is lenient or inconsistent, it will fuel your child's OCD and leave him even more confused than ever.

Our brains are designed to form behavior and habits and stick to them. Whenever you try to change a behavior, it is often replaced by something else. You need to be mindful that your child hasn't shifted from one OCD ritual to another. So, be a vigilant parent and alert all the primary caregivers in his life about the same. A little vigilance goes a long way while helping your child tackle

OCD.

Apart from all the different tips discussed in the section, another simple thing you need to remember is to be mindful of your own OCD behaviors. If you are diagnosed with OCD or have mild tendencies that resonate with OCD, seek the help you need. By modeling desirable behavior, the risk of reinforcing your child's OCD reduces. You might need to seek professional help to help your child manage his OCD. If your child is getting treated for it, ensure that you are 100% involved in his treatment.

Tips to Deal With Post-Traumatic Stress Disorder

Post-traumatic stress disorder or PTSD, as the name suggests, is a condition that develops after suffering through a traumatic event. If your child has undergone a traumatic event recently, you need to comfort, support, and reassure him that he's safe. You should also provide him the same to help manage his fears, grief, and recover healthily. In this section, let's look at some simple tips all parents can use to help that kid with PTSD.

The first thing you need to do is ensure that your child feels safe. Whether he is a toddler or a preschooler, going the extra mile to make him feel safe and comfortable is important. Whether it is an extra hug or a reassuring pat on the back, these simple gestures will make him feel more safe and secure. This is quite important, especially after he has witnessed a frightening or disturbing event.

Children, regardless of their age, look to their parents for comfort, support, and reassurance. This is even more important after a traumatic event. So, you need to stay calm and composed. If you have anxiety or worries about something, keep them to yourself for now. Unlike the other anxiety-related disorders, your child will not benefit from knowing that you are anxious too. Amidst all the chaos, he's looking to you for comfort. Whenever your child is around, be mindful of your voice and behavior.

Try to maintain a routine as much as you possibly can. Routines might sound boring, but they are comforting and predictable for a child. When he knows what has to be done and when, it brings with it a sense of security. Routines also reassure your child. Whether it is regular bedtime or mealtime, ensure that you follow this routine.

Yes, it was mentioned that you should not share your anxieties with your child for now, but talking about the event helps. Talk to your child about what happened, how it felt, and reassure him that it is okay. Learning the details of a dramatic event from an adult he trusts can work wonders for his mental health right now. Learn to be honest while having this discussion. Also, be brief and don't go into any worrying details. At the same time, encourage your child to ask more questions about what happened. The more information he has, the better equipped he is to deal with the stressful experiences. Don't leave any unnecessary gaps in his imagination that might conjure wild scenarios. Instead, replace it with realistic thoughts and facts. The information you share needs to be age appropriate and something that your child can handle and manage.

Encourage your child to enjoy himself. Just because he has suffered a traumatic event doesn't mean he needs to stop enjoying his life. Create a positive environment at home and maintain it. Encourage your child to go out, play, and engage with others of his age, and offer him distractions. This distraction brings with it a sense of normalcy that is desirable for children.

Since your child has recently experienced a traumatic event, it is important to prevent his exposure to further trauma. Whether it is news about a specific incident on the TV, social media, or anywhere else, ensure that his exposure to any disturbing news is limited. Limiting the exposure to news coverage at this stage can be quite good. It helps him understand that the traumatic event was only temporary and not a permanent fixture in his life.

Try to understand that all children are unique and they use different coping mechanisms. If your child wants to spend some more time with his friends or needs some space and time for himself, indulge him. It is okay. You don't know what your child is truly experiencing right now. Another simple technique you can use is to talk to him about his feelings. Reassure him that any anger, mistrust, fear, guilt, or sadness he experiences is normal. Some might cry when they're sad or throw a tantrum when angry. Try to accommodate him without going overboard. If it means letting your child cry once in a while, it is okay. Don't force him to do something he doesn't want to. Don't force him to pretend that everything is okay when he's not feeling fine. Also start to normalize emotions and feelings.

Be a good listener. Don't give in to the temptation of lecturing him about what he's supposed to are not supposed to feel. If the event feels overwhelming to him, he will act out. Don't be angry and instead, try to understand how your child is viewing the situation. Adults don't realize it, but children view the same situation quite differently. By understanding his perspective, you get a better sense of why he is worried. This gives you more information about what you can do to ease his worries.

Don't dismiss his feelings and instead acknowledge them. If your child admits he's worried or concerned about something, don't brush it off and tell him that he shouldn't be. Do not embarrass or criticize him or his feelings and thoughts. Instead, create an open environment in the house so that he knows he can come to you in time of his need. At times, a simple acknowledgment of his worries will reduce and ease his fears.

At times, he might ask questions that you don't know the answers to. There can also be instances when you don't know how to respond. In such situations, understand that it is perfectly all right to say that you don't know. You can always get back to your child later. Instead of giving him a wrong answer or filling his head with misinformation, it's better to take your time and get back to him later.

Apart from all these different tips and techniques, you need to help your child relax. Practicing relaxing activities such as listening to music, impromptu exercise, progressive muscle relaxation, and deep breathing can help. You will learn in detail about all these different relaxation techniques later in this book. For now, understand that you need to set some time aside for teaching and practicing these relaxation techniques to your child.

Chapter eight

Strategies to Support An Anxious Child

As a parent, it is your natural tendency to go into a protective mode when your child's anxiety is heightened. You might try to solve his problems or help him in any way to avoid all triggers of anxiety. Chances are you have tried to engineer a lifestyle that's worry-free for him. You are doing all this to help your child avoid his anxiety. Regardless of how well-meaning your intentions are, all this is counterproductive. The best way to teach a child to manage and overcome his anxiety is by equipping him with the required skills and tools to do this. Instead of solving his problems or helping him avoid anxiety, teach him to manage them. After all, the hard truth of life that all parents need to accept at one point or another is that they cannot protect their child all the time. In this section, let's look at some simple and practical strategies you can use to support your child.

Start With Clear Expectations

The sooner you normalize anxiety, the better it is for your child's wellbeing. Stop treating his anxiety like a disability. Don't offer any unnecessary special considerations. Ensure that the expectations for an anxious child are similar to those of a non-anxious child. At the same time, you should also make certain allowances and accommodations to proceed slowly. For instance, children might be quite excited at the prospect of attending parties and spending a lot of time with peers. If your anxious child wants some quiet time to himself and wants to get away from crowds, let him do that. Never force your child to do things he is not yet ready to. It is good to be encouraging and supportive, but there is a fine line between supportive and pushing. Instead of overwhelming a child, concentrate on taking small steps.

By establishing clear expectations, it helps create appropriate benchmarks for your child to reach such expectations. This will give him a chance to finally work through his anxious feelings without getting overwhelmed. It also teaches him to manage anxiety.

Don't Avoid

Whatever you do, avoid avoidance at all costs. Avoiding your child's anxiety triggers will not do anyone any favors. You might think you're protecting him, but you are merely raising a child who is poorly equipped to deal with anxiety. Remember, anxiety will not go away until he learns to manage it. If you are failing to teach him how to manage it, sooner or later he'll get overwhelmed. For instance, if your child experiences anxiety whenever he sees a dog, the solution is not to avoid all dogs. If avoiding all dogs is the solution, it merely validates his anxious thoughts. It might wrongly convey the message to your child that all dogs are dangerous animals and should be avoided at all costs. Refrain from engaging in behaviors that further strengthen his anxious thoughts. Instead, work on desensitizing him. To desensitize his anxiety triggers, you need to take small steps.

Let us go back to the previous example of anxiety around dogs. If that's the case, you can start with a virtual environment where your child gets a chance to desensitize his fears. Perhaps you can sit together and look at different breeds of dogs online. You might also consider watching some funny or cute videos to make your child more comfortable. While you are doing this, ensure that you are talking about his anxiety and its triggers. Once he is comfortable doing these things, you could take him to the local dog park, stand at a distance, and let him observe dogs while they play. The final step is to encourage him to meet a friendly dog.

Tackling anxiety is not something that can be achieved overnight. Instead, it is a collection of small steps taken over a prolonged period. Always look at the bigger picture while helping your child manage his anxiety. He can learn a lot from his worries and fears. During the stage, your only role is to act as a guide and mentor. Apart from this, give him the support and encouragement required to take these small steps.

Worrying is Not Bad

It was previously mentioned that you should never tell an anxious child to stop worrying. You're also given suggestions about what you can say instead. No one, regardless of whether they're an adult or child, has ever stopped worrying because someone else told them to. When it comes to worries, it is always a personal decision whether you want to indulge it or not. If your child is worrying about something, don't brush his worries aside, ridicule them, or tell them they are meaningless or irrelevant. Instead, set some time aside for him to worry. Give him some worry time daily. Tell him he's free to worry for 20 minutes daily and that's it. During these 20 minutes, sit with him, make a list of his worries, the reasons, and how these worries make him feel. A great way to elevate anxiety is by talking about it. Give him some uninterrupted time to vent his worries without any judgment. While your child is talking, don't interrupt and instead play the role of a good listener. After this, you can sit together and brainstorm some solutions.

Anxiety Coping Kit

Equipping your child with a variety of coping mechanisms and skills is the best way to empower him to control his worries. An efficient technique is to create a list of strategies you can use whenever anxiety strikes. Spend some time, brainstorm simple ideas, and make a note of them. Encourage him to carry this note with him wherever he goes. Alternatively, you can help him memorize the list. Some simple activities you can include in his anxiety coping kit are progressive muscle relaxation, writing about his worries, taking a couple of deep breaths, using a stress ball, talking about his worries, and reframing his thoughts. Encourage him to get help from an adult if his anxiety becomes too much.

Reframing Anxious Thoughts

The thought cycle of anxiety is overwhelming. Whether you are a child or an adult, it never stops being overwhelming. Anxiety increases the feeling of helplessness. Your child unknowingly gets caught in the trap of pondering about all the "what ifs" and "I cant's" as soon as his anxiety spikes. Anxiety-ridden children usually have a black-or-white, all-or-nothing attitude. They are adept at overgeneralizing. This is incredibly problematic. Life cannot be classified as either black or white. For an anxious mind, there are always opposites that exist. For instance, an anxious mind might assume that someone was laughing at them instead of a situation. This worsens the anxiety he might already be experiencing.

A simple yet effective way to strengthen your child's thinking, increase realistic thought patterns, and reduce negativity is by practicing reframing anxious thoughts. Yes, anxious thoughts can be efficiently reframed. After all, they are triggered by uncomfortable thoughts, feelings, and emotions. To do this, set some time aside daily and work on positive reframing with your child. It might not be easy during the initial stages, but it is effective.

For positive reframing, here are some simple questions you can ask your child.

- Is there anything that you are worried about right now?
- What does this worry make you feel?
- What does this specific worry tell you?

- Do you think this worry is genuine? Why don't we see whether it is right or wrong?
- How can we change this thought into something more positive?

As human beings, we all live in groups and crave our peers' approval. It increases the sense of belonging and togetherness. A common fear anxious children have is the fear of being disliked or excluded. If your child is expressing this worry, it is time to help reframe this worry positively. Ask him why he believes this. Perhaps there was some incident at school which formed this thought. Let's assume that your child didn't know the answer to a question when he was asked. As he was fumbling for words, another kid laughed at him. Remember, you are dealing with children here. Your child's peers don't yet have emotional intelligence. After such an incident, your child might be harboring the anxiety that he's disliked at school. Now that you know what his worry is, how it makes him feel, and how it cropped up, it's time to break down the reality of the situation. Ask him about his usual participation in the class. Ask him about his favorite parts of school activities. Ask him more questions to understand your child's life at school. After this, help reframe his anxious thoughts into something more positive. Help him reframe the situation as follows. "I was hurt when the other kid laughed at me, but it doesn't mean I don't have any other friends at school." Or "I know I felt bad when the kid laughed at me, but there are several other things I enjoy at school." This simple exercise is all about reframing his thoughts and ideas for the better. Instead of fixating on the negative experience, you are helping him concentrate on something more positive. Focusing on the positive helps reduce the power of a negative or anxious thought.

Practice a Little Empathy

Anxiety can be frightening and paralyzing to a certain extent for children. When a child is overwhelmed by his anxious thoughts, performing everyday actions like attending school, mingling with his peers, or playing a sport can also become difficult. It's not uncommon for anxious children to avoid activities that promote uncomfortable thoughts and feelings. They start withdrawing, and when this happens, their discomfort further heightens. Why does this happen? It's because they are seeing their peers do things they are struggling with. It can make them feel like an outsider.

If you notice your child is avoiding fun activities because he's worried about his anxiety, it's time to step in. No, it doesn't mean you push and force him to do things that trigger his anxiety. Instead, it means you become more empathizing and encouraging. By telling him that he is not alone and you understand what he's feeling, the feeling of alienation he might be experiencing will reduce. Normalizing his anxiety will make him feel better. Repeatedly remind him that he is not alone and that you are there with him. If he seems worried about attending a party, instead of forcing him to go, off er some helpful alternatives. For instance, you can tell him, "Why don't you go for an hour and see if you like it?" or "It might be fun to step outside for a while and play with your friends!" You can also tell him, "Mommy will come and get you if you get uncomfortable," or "This is the perfect time to practice anxietycoping mechanisms we were talking about."

Concentrate on the Basics

Concentrating on your child's basic health is important. If he's physically fi t and healthy, his ability to regulate anxiety increases. He doesn't have to attend all parties or play every sport at school.

He does need to slow down and concentrate on maintaining his health. The basic components you need to be mindful of are sleep, a healthy diet, and plenty of hydration. Apart from those, add some form of physical exercise to his daily routine. Whether it is riding his bike, playing at the park, or engaging in any sport he likes, he needs to stay physically fit. Schedule some downtime into his daily routine too. At the end of the day, give him some time to decompress and relax. Another simple aspect of his lifestyle you need to concentrate on is spending time outdoors. Encourage him to spend some time outdoors, whether it is to play or relax.

All the simple strategies discussed in this section make you a mindful parent while helping your child tackle his anxiety. Start incorporating the suggestions slowly into your parenting practices. It will take conscious effort and consistency, but your efforts will be worth it.

CHAPTER NINE

How to Help Your Child
Manage Fears

Fears are an inescapable part of human nature. Regardless of whether you are old or young, we all have our fears. They are an unavoidable part of childhood too. Whether it is hiding under the blankets when lightning strikes, behind the couch during a thunderstorm, or hiding from the boogeyman in the closet, children are scared of different things. Here is one scenario that sounds quite familiar to parents—it is time for your little one to go to bed. You have performed all the nightly routines, read him a bedtime story, tucked him in for a good night's sleep, and as you are about to switch off the light, he says, "Mommy can I have another glass of water?" or "Can I have five minutes before I sleep?"

Why is the child doing all this? Perhaps he's scared of sleeping alone! All this is normal.

When your child is scared, the parental instant might be to comfort him. Reassure him there are no monsters in the closet, there is no boogeyman, and so on. Ideally, refrain from doing this. You might want to comfort him, but in the long run, this is not an ideal way to go about parenting him. Instead of teaching him to overcome his fears, you are merely fueling them. It might be quite cute if a three-year-old is worried about a monster under her bed, but if a 13-year-old does this, it's not age-appropriate. The best gift any parent can give to their kid is self-confidence. If you want to raise a confident child who is not always anxious, you need to reduce parental intervention. A little less parental intervention means more independence and confidence as he grows up. He will also feel more in control of his thoughts, feelings and emotions. In the section, let's look at some simple practices you can follow to help your child manage his fears.

Fill in the Missing Pieces

Children are still trying to understand the ways of the world. Only now are they beginning to comprehend the relationship between cause and effect. This relationship isn't obvious to them yet, and they are slowly learning. For instance, a child might be scared that if he plays too close to the vacuum cleaner, he will be sucked into it. It might seem quite obvious to an adult, but not so much to a child. By filling in the missing pieces of information, you help him get a better understanding of what is happening and the reasons for the same. For instance, you can show him how the vacuum cleaner works. Tell him that a button might be picked up by the machine but a shoe or a stuffed toy will not. So, obviously, a person cannot be sucked into it. Offering information helps the child rationalize what is happening. It can reduce their fears and anxieties too.

Concentrate on the Present

Most of the fears and anxieties children harbor are a combination of the past and the future. For instance, if a child is scared of dogs, it is probably because of a past incident where he was either chased by one or was barked at. This probably scared him. His brain might create a relationship between this past and a future incident such as a dog bite. Now, your child has not experienced it, yet his brain believes it can happen. This is the reason for his fear. By pulling him back to the present, you are preventing his brain from getting over-excited and worried about the future. This is especially true when your child starts generalizing different fears. Even though the incidents might seem similar, generalization is harmful. By teaching him the difference between different things, it reduces the intensity of the fear.

Don't Overreact

Whatever you do, do not overreact. Don't dismiss or invalidate your child's fears. Whatever he's feeling, it is quite real for him. For instance, if your kid is scared there is a monster hiding in the closet or under his bed, scooping him up and comforting him merely reinforces the presence of fear. Unknowingly, you are conveying the message that there is something to be scared of. Apart from this, you are also sending him a message that he will be safe in your arms. So the next time he is scared, he will expect you to pick him up. This shouldn't be his go-to solution whenever he's scared. A cuddle can be a reward, but it shouldn't be a reward for an avoidant behavior. Instead of comforting him, gently talk to him about what is happening. If he's scared of the sound the balloon makes when it pops, tell him what happened. After this, empathize with the fact that he got scared when the balloon popped. Talking about fear takes away its power. It will also make him more comfortable to approach you in the future and talk about his fears.

Storytelling Helps

Regardless of how irrational your child's fear or anxiety might seem, there is usually a rational story behind that fear. Any generalization he draws between different fears is automatic. A common generalization is "all dogs are bad" or "all dogs will hurt me." A simple way to interrupt this generalization is by focusing on the initial event that led to this manifestation. Stories are a part of our life. We use them to connect with others, heal, and expand our horizons and knowledge.

The right hemisphere of the brain is responsible for all your emotions and memories while the left hemisphere is the center for logic, factual details, and rationalization. Both these sides need to work in tandem or else you will experience the feeling of disconnection. A simple way to reestablish the link between both these hemispheres is via storytelling. The right brain usually becomes quite dominant whenever you experience any fear. This reaction is automatic. By reintroducing the left brain into the picture, intense fear is slowly replaced by rationalization. To do this, you need to consciously work on reintroducing the left brain by encouraging your child to tell his story. Next time, if your child says he is scared of dogs or all dogs are out to get him, ask him why he feels so. Encourage him to narrate the first incident that led to this fear. If he says something like, "I know dogs are dangerous because I've seen it," or "Dogs can hurt people," it is his right brain that is talking.

Once your child has narrated his story, encourage the participation of his right hemisphere by asking him specific questions. Ask him about what he felt during the experience or the different **feelings he experiences whenever he is in a similar situation. If you see that your child is visibly scared or frightened while talking about his fears, state it. When you name an emotion, emotional intensity reduces. By encouraging a conversation about how his fears came into being, their power over him will reduce. When you talk about something that bothers you, the problem seems simpler and easier. If you don't talk about a** specific experience or your child avoids talking about it, sooner **or later those unprocessed thoughts and feelings will manifest** themselves differently. If such unprocessed thoughts come to the **forefront, they can manifest as anxiety. They might also present themselves as nightmares or recurring dreams. To avoid all this, try the simple activity of storytelling.**

Reworking the Association

Fears are associated with feelings and memories. If these fears are intense, they are automatically associated with powerful feelings, emotions, and memories that are often bad. By reworking this association, you can reduce the fear your child feels. Concentrate on reworking the association by forming a new relationship with these fears. Instead of bad feelings and memories, replace them with fun and relaxing activities. For instance, if your child is extremely scared of thunderstorms, start by acknowledging his fears. Let him know it is normal and validated. After this, it is time to redirect him towards fun and relaxing activities such as watching a movie, coloring, or even listening to music. Once he's ready, you can turn it into a joke. Whenever there is lightning or thunder, someone has to crack a funny joke or play a peppy song. By doing this, you are essentially eliminating the scary thoughts or feelings and memories while replacing them with positive associations. After a while, this reduces the negative associations and replaces them with positive feelings that your child welcomes.

Stepladder Technique

This is a common technique used in therapy to reduce and overcome fears. It is based on the idea of gradually and gently exposing your child to an object or situation he's scared of. This slow and gradual exposure reduces his sensitivity to the trigger of fear and helps teach them a better response. When a child is scared of something, the object or situation seems quite scary and overwhelming. In such scenarios, your child would want to avoid said trigger as much as he possibly can. By slowly familiarizing him with the trigger, it increases his confidence. He will also feel less helpless and more empowered when faced with his fears. One thing you should remember while using this technique is to be slow and gradual. Remember the mantra" slow and steady wins the race" while using the stepladder technique. If your child is not yet ready, don't push him more than he can handle. It will prove counterproductive. Here are the simple steps you need to follow to use the stepladder technique.

Talk to Your Child

Before you implement this plan, you must discuss it with your kid. Unless he is on board with this plan, it will not work. After all, he is the hero of the story. You should also reassure him that he has complete control over what will be done and when to stop. This reassurance helps improve his confi dence while facing the fear. Also, don't forget to remind him that you will never do anything that would harm him or his safety.

Let's assume that your child is really scared of dogs. Now, the idea is to help this fear and eliminate it if possible. To do this, it's time to start a conversation about dogs. Start by telling him you understand he's scared of dogs and the reasons why he's scared of them. After this, tell him not all dogs are generally scary. Your child might be worried that any dog he comes across will hurt him. His brain might start sounding alarm bells. Reassure and empathize that you understand his worries. Tell him it is not his fault for thinking so. Talk to him about how he feels when he's scared and how the fear controls him. Remind him that he's the boss of his brain. He can tell his brain what it needs to think.

Before you start explaining what the stepladder is, tell him you both will not be doing anything he doesn't want to. Don't forget to reassure him that you both will never do anything that can harm him. At the same time, remind him he needs to show a little courage to tackle his fear. Reassure him once again that the decision is truly his. Never underestimate the importance of reassurance while reframing what your child feels. After this, it is time to explain how this technique will work.

Explanation Time

Even if your child isn't fully on board with the idea yet, he might be slightly curious or fascinated by what you have in mind. Once he is open to listening to how this technique works, start talking about it. Perhaps you can use an example of something children are usually scared of but your kid is not. Constantly remind him there will always be an out and you can stop working on this technique whenever he wants. If you force him to do something or if he feels forced to, his fight-or-flight response will kick in and the fear can turn into anxiety. If this happens, his brain will forget about all logical reasoning and explanations. Instead, it will only receive information that he needs to get away from the situation and avoid it.

Talk to your child calmly and reassuringly. Start with an example of something that other kids are usually scared of, such as heights. Tell him that whatever you are saying is just an explanation and it doesn't mean he needs to follow it. This conversation can go something like this: "Do you know that a lot of children are scared of heights? Well, imagine how scary slippery slides might be for them. Imagine all the fun they are missing out on because they are scared of heights! What do you think such a child can do to make himself feel more comfortable with the slippery slide? How can he get used to being higher on the ladder?"

When you ask your child these questions, chances are he'll come up with a couple of answers. Keep an open mind to all the answers your child has, regardless of how quirky they sound. The idea of this process is to help him plan and analyze the activity at hand. This simple process helps strengthen all the different connections in his prefrontal cortex responsible for keeping his brain calm during anxiety.

Now, your child might have some interesting responses. Perhaps the most common response is, "Why doesn't the child try climbing one step at a time? Once he gets used to it, he can climb a little higher!" If your child comes up with this, your job just becomes a lot easier. On the other hand, chances are your child might also say something along the lines of, "If he's so scared of heights, stay away from slippery slides altogether. He doesn't need them!" Before you start shaking your head in resignation, accept your child's answer and offer some positive prompting. Perhaps you can suggest that the child in the hypothetical scenario should take it one step at a time and see how he feels.

Make It a Little Personal

If your child understands the idea of slow, gentle, or gradual exposure, start talking to him about his fears. Ask him what he would like to do to tackle these fears. Before you make any suggestions, ask him what he would be okay with. Try to understand that something is truly problematic only when that prevents him from leading his life like he's supposed to. If required, offer gentle prompts. Instead of telling him that he is suffering from anxiety or getting into its nuances, why don't you ask him how he would feel if he was not worried all the time? This can be a conversation starter. While talking about this, reassure him that he's quite brave and he has the power to stop his worries.

Simplify It

Fear can be quite overwhelming. A simple way to make it seem more manageable is by breaking it into smaller steps and worries. You and your child should be equally involved in this process. His willingness to commit to the suggestions or implement any of the proposed ideas is dependent on his level of involvement. Ensure the first step to tackle the fear is quite easy and it's something your child can do independently.

For instance, if your child is worried about sleeping on his own, work with him to create a plan of action. Perhaps the first step can be to leave the night light on for a while longer. You can stay with him for another 10 minutes before going to your room, or even check on him once every 10 minutes. Once he has cleared this stage, increase the time limit of checking on him to 20 minutes. Do this slowly until your child can successfully sleep through the night. It is doable, but it is not an overnight process. It will take plenty of time and attention. In the meanwhile, be patient.

Let us go back to the earlier example of a child who is scared of dogs. Now, you need to establish a simplified stepladder that can be used to conquer the fear of dogs. The easiest step should be at the bottom of the ladder while the hardest is at the top. If the child is scared of dogs, the first step can be to look at pictures of dogs. The second step might be to touch a soft toy and play with it. The third step can be watching a movie about a happy and friendly dog. The fourth step might be to stand in front of a dog without getting scared. The fifth step can be touching the dog, and the sixth step can be holding the dog for a while longer. Once the child is comfortable with a small dog, he can be encouraged to repeat the same process with a bigger dog.

The Rule About Small Steps

While breaking the fear into different steps, the distance between the two steps needs to be quite small. If the steps are too far apart, he can get overwhelmed. The smaller the distance, the easier it is for the child to move ahead. For instance, in the previous example, if the first step is to look at pictures of dogs and the second step is to hold a real dog, the chances of anxiety creeping in are quite high.

Don't Be In a Rush

Never forget that you are dealing with a child. Take as much time as he needs to comfortably make his way through the stepladder. Don't be in a rush. This is not a process that can be rushed. If you try to rush it, you will worsen your child's fear or anxiety. Don't forget to congratulate your child whenever he takes a step. Positive reinforcement and feedback will increase motivation to try the next step. If he needs a little push, offer encouragement, but don't be forceful. Forcing your child to do something he's not yet ready to do will increase anxiety.

CHAPTER TEN

How to Teach Positive
Thinking to Tackle Anxiety

When your child's worrying thoughts become excessive, his ability to cope with them reduces. From poor sleep to reduced attention and reluctance to do things outside his comfort zone, there are different problems associated with anxiety. A powerful technique you can use to help your child overcome his worries is to teach him to think realistically. The process is quite simple. You essentially teach him how to identify a worrying thought, look for any evidence to support the thought, and if there is no evidence, replace it with something more realistic. This is an essential part of cognitive-behavioral therapy discussed in the previous chapter. It teaches him to reframe all his negative thoughts, behaviors, and emotions and transform them into something more positive and realistic.

It might sound like positive thinking, but it is not. The worrying thoughts are replaced with realistic ones instead of positive ones. If you want to teach your child this technique, here are the steps you should follow.

The first step is perhaps the most difficult one. Start by identifying his thoughts. Tell him thoughts are nothing more than words we say to ourselves. These words don't have to be said out loud, but we think them. An average brain thinks thousands of thoughts daily. Most of these are automatic and are similar to the blowing wind. Merely identifying a thought can be quite empowering for the child.

You can try playing some simple games to help your child identify his thoughts. For instance, if you are watching a movie, cartoon, or even looking at pictures in a book, ask him what those people might be thinking. Encourage him to guess what those characters might be thinking. Alternatively, you can give him a situation or an event and ask what a specific person might be feeling. For instance, if he is scared of dogs, ask him what his beloved character would think or feel in a situation when a dog is present in front of him. Ask him to draw what he's thinking or name the thought.

Depending on his age, you can also go ahead and explain the connection between our thoughts, feelings, and behaviors. For instance, any thought that worries us can cause butterflies in our stomachs. This feeling increases the temptation to avoid the situation that's causing the worry. You must spend some time and help him accurately identify his worry. If he's scared of the dark, chances are he will tell you he is experiencing an emotion instead of the thought. A sentence such as "I'm scared of the dark" identifies his feelings. The feeling is fear. You will need to probe a little deep and ask him what exactly about the dark scares him. This helps identify the worrying thought.

Once he has identified his worry, encourage him to gather the required evidence to support his thought. Tell him he's playing the role of a detective and looking for clues to support his thought. You can also ask him simple questions in this activity.

If he is scared of the dark, ask him, "What about the dark scares you?" If he says he's worried about a boogeyman in the closet or a monster under his bed, ask him how likely is that a boogeyman is present in the closet or a monster is hiding under his bed. Ask him how he will feel about the same worry a couple of weeks later. Or maybe you can ask him what his favorite character or even best friend would do in a similar situation.

After going through this activity, chances are your child's worry is not founded in reality. If that's the case, you need to teach him to replace this worrying thought with something more realistic. If he hears a creepy sound right before going to bed, instead of assuming it's a monster under the bed, ask him what it can be. If he's struggling to answer, offer some helpful suggestions such as the rustling of the wind or any other noise coming from outside.

Once you have followed all these steps, chances are your child's fear will have been replaced with something more realistic. This is one activity you need to perform repeatedly to help him overcome his fears. Changing his thinking pattern is not an overnight process. To do this, you need to regularly talk to him about what he's feeling and what is going on in his head. Regular check-ins will encourage him to open up about his worries. If you are an empathetic listener, he will talk more about his worries without the fear of judgment.

Whenever possible, talk to him about emotions and correctly identify his thoughts. Encourage him to tell you what exactly he is worried about instead of stating his emotions.

After this, teach him to think more realistically with examples. An ideal way to do this is by modeling the behavior you want him to learn. After all, parents are a child's first role model. By incorporating fun activities and games into this process, you make realistic thinking fun and exciting. It's also a great way to bond with your little one.

Chapter eleven

Self -Soothing Techniques for Kids with Anxiety

It's not likely that you will be with your child whenever he experiences anxiety. So, you need to equip him with certain skills and tools he can use whenever anxiety strikes. Let's look at some simple activities your child can perform anywhere and at any time to gain better control of his senses and relax.

Deep Breathing

When your child is anxious, his breathing becomes rapid and shallow. A simple way to counteract this anxiety response is by regulating his breathing. Encourage your child to take calm, slow, and deep breaths whenever he's anxious. This reduces the feeling of stress. The activity he needs to perform is quite simple. Ask him to breathe slowly and deeply through his nose, hold onto this breath for a second or two before exhaling through his mouth. Encourage him to repeat this process five to 10 times or until he feels calmer. According to the research conducted by Valentina Perciavalle et al. (2017), deep breathing reduces stress in any situation.

A Mental Vacation

A simple way to help your child let go of his anxiety is by encouraging him to take a mental vacation. Even if he cannot physically distance himself from the stressor, ask him to close his eyes and think of his favorite place. Whether it is the beach, park, or the mountains, ask him to visualize his favorite place. If not, ask him to think about his favorite memory—perhaps the family vacation or even a visit to Disneyland. By visualizing his favorite destination, his anxious mind will become calm. Depending on your child's age, ask him to make his visualization quite realistic. From how he felt on a specific day or at that place to the different smells, sounds, and sights, encourage him to think about all of it.

Head to Toe Relaxations

According to the research conducted by Maryam Zargardzadeh (2014), progressive muscle relaxation reduces anxiety. Even though the subjects of this study were nursing students, there's no reason why it wouldn't stand true for kids. A method to do relaxation or progressive relaxation is the next step of deep breathing. Ask your child to find a quiet spot for himself and place a hand on his tummy and another on his chest. Ask him to close his eyes and keep breathing slowly and deeply until his entire body feels calm. This reduces muscle tension and calms his mind. When his body is physically calm, his mind will slowly calm down too.

Holding on Tight

Anxiety triggers muscle tension. This is an involuntary consequence of the stress response. A simple way to help your child counteract this involuntary muscle tension is by holding on tight or squeezing something. Whether it is modeling clay, a stuffed animal, or a stress ball, the action of holding tight reduces tension. It also diverts your child's mind from the anxious thought and helps him concentrate on something else.

A Positive Thought

In the previous chapter, you were introduced to diff erent steps you can follow to teach your child realistic thinking. Now, it is time to encourage him to replace his worrying and negative thoughts with positive ones. If your child is anxious about meeting new people or scared of trying something new, ask him to replace these thoughts with positive ones. For instance, if he believes that he cannot do something, encourage him to think, "I can do it," or "I am strong enough to do it." If he keeps repeating these positive thoughts like a mantra, it distracts the mind and encourages relaxation.

A Little Movement

According to the research conducted by Elizabeth Anderson et al. (2013), physical movement and activity reduce anxiety and stress response. Whenever your child is anxious, encourage him to engage in a little physical activity. Whether it is jumping on the spot for a minute or two or running three laps in the yard or the playground, some form of physical movement helps. When he gets his body moving, feel-good endorphins are released that reduce the presence of cortisol in his body.

Listening to Music

Music has a therapeutic and calming effect on the mind. According to the research conducted by Myrian V. Thoma et al. (2013), listening to music reduces the intensity and duration of the stress response. The next time your child feels anxious, encourage him to listen to his favorite song. If he cannot do this, ask him to sing or hum his favorite song. If possible, an impromptu dance party in the living room will act as a great stress buster.

Apart from all these self-soothing techniques, there's another important tip you need to remember. Dear parents, be a good role model for your child. How you deal with your anxiety and stress sets the tone for how your child learns to cope with them. The next time you feel overwhelmed, anxious, or worried, explain what you're feeling. Instead of letting your emotions get the better of you and acting out, calmly state what you are feeling. When you are anxious, having an outburst is quite likely. Instead of an outburst, say something like, "I have so many things to complete and I'm worried that I cannot complete. I just need to take a break for a minute until I feel better."

Chapter twelve

Anxiety Relapse

The joy of truly knowing that your child is free from symptoms of anxiety and can manage his emotions and feelings positively is quite exhilarating. No one will want their child's anxiety to relapse. While your child is learning to manage his anxiety, you might be waiting for the other shoe to drop. Bracing yourself for any hint of anxiety to return is anxiety-inducing for parents. Unfortunately, there are instances when there can be a relapse. Even if your child has been coping incredibly well with his anxiety, the chances of a relapse are possible. It can be quite exhausting and overwhelming to think you need to repeat everything you've done until now all over again. So, it's always better to prepare yourself for the reasons that can trigger anxiety relapse. When you know what needs to be avoided, taking corrective action before it manifests into a problem becomes easier. In this chapter, you will learn about some causes of relapse of anxiety in children and what to do in case of a relapse.

Causes of a Relapse

It might have been a while since your child faced his original fear. All of a sudden, an event or an occurrence triggers his fear again. Let's assume that your child had an intense fear of spiders and managed to overcome it. After a couple of months, you are all watching some movie about spiders and it triggers his phobia again. Or perhaps your child was dealing with separation anxiety. He managed to overcome it, and after a while, there was an unforeseeable circumstance where you were separated from your child. This can trigger a relapse of his fear. There can also be an environmental change in the household that is traumatic for the child. Dealing with an illness, the death of a loved one, or shifting to a new place can be quite stressful and anxietyinducing for children. If any such events occur, the chances of relapse also increase.

If there are any significant changes in the situation surrounding the fear, there can be a relapse. For instance, your child might have been quite scared about starting elementary school. From social anxiety to separation anxiety, he experienced it all. He managed his anxiety and got used to the school. Everything was going well until he had to start middle school. As the date approached, his anxiety returned. This is quite possible.

There can be situations where your child's anxiety levels are better but he still prefers to play it safe. For instance, he might be quite anxious about whether all the doors and windows are locked and secured at night. He might have learned to stop indulging in this obsessive behavior or compulsion of checking the doors and windows every night. That said, it doesn't mean he will not ask for reassurance that everything is properly taken care of. If he constantly asks for this reassurance even though he is not engaging in the compulsive behavior, it is a sign his anxiety has returned.

Any situation of unrelated anxiety or stress can trigger his previous anxieties. Simply put, when your child faces a traumatic incident or a frightening situation, his anxiety can return. For instance, a child who has learned to manage his fear of dogs and gets over it can have a relapse upon hearing that one of his friends was bitten by a dog.

What to Do Now?

If you are working with your child to reduce his anxiety and it returns, it can be quite stressful for you. Regardless of the combination of treatments you are using to help your child manage his anxiety, whenever it relapses, you need to go back to the basics. Anxiety can be quite stubborn and the fears are never truly forgotten. Relapse is similar to an old memory which is once again remembered vividly. During a relapse, the goal is not to reduce your child's anxiety but disprove his fear once again. Once the fear goes away, the anxiety will also reduce.

It's time to go back to the basics. Start identifying all those beliefs your child is harboring and paying attention to once again. It's time to challenge all of them. Practice the different **tips** discussed in the previous chapter about helping your **child** face and manage his fears. If you believe any specific incident or **situation is triggering his anxiety,** give him a break from it. Once your child has managed to identify his fear, you can start again. In this section, let's look at simple tips you can follow if your child has a relapse.

The first step is you have to be calm. Do not lose your patience and do not get upset with your child. It is incredibly frustrating for him to go through the same things he has already lived through. It can be frustrating for you and it is understandable. It is equally understandable that your child is frustrated too. You need to stay calm right now.

Concentrate on teaching him to develop his confidence. Give him the confidence and support required to keep going without giving up. He's counting on you for all of this. Don't lose hope; be his cheerleader.

If one of his previous fears has become active now, it is time to face it. The sooner you accept it, the easier it is to face the fear. Challenge his fears instead of avoiding or ignoring them. Encourage your child to do the same. It might seem easy to ignore or avoid the fear because it is triggering his anxiety, but don't do this. Reassure him that you are there with him and he can manage this fear too.

While you are helping your child face his fear, ensure that you don't stop once it eases. Instead, it's time to go all the way. Relapses are common. Things can get better, but it doesn't mean the anxiety goes away. If you realize his anxiety is once again interfering with his daily life and preventing him from living his life to the fullest, it's time to tackle it. Face all the fears, revisit them, and help him challenge them. Follow the tips discussed in the previous chapters to do this.

Apart from this, consult his healthcare provider about the relapse immediately. If required, restart cognitive behavioral therapy once again. Whether it is therapy or medication, ensure you get him the required help.

Chapter thirteen

Parents Should Not Pass on Their Anxiety to Kids

Consider this scenario. A parent was trying to get her kid to his softball practice. Before leaving the house, she got an important call from work that delayed her attempts to get to the practice on time. She was anxious about her work and didn't check whether her kid was wearing his softball uniform or not. On the way to the practice, she noticed he was not dressed for practice. She felt frustrated and overwhelmed and ended up shouting at her kid for not being ready on time.

What do you think is wrong in this situation? The mother was unknowingly projecting her anxiety and frustration on her kid. She didn't make sure whether he was dressed for the practice or not before leaving home. She was transferring her anxiety to her kid, who became the unintended victim of her outburst.

Now, consider the same situation from the child's perspective. The child might believe he was shouted at because he wasn't dressed properly. Whenever he needs to go out, he might become anxious wondering whether or not he is dressed according to what his parents want. He might also develop some irrational fears associated with this incident. In the situation mentioned above, the child was not scared of his mother, but of the negative reaction. He might believe he had upset his mother. Children expect their parents to be their rock. Seeing their solid pillar of support crumble under pressure sends the wrong message.

What is the moral of this story? The moral is quite simple— don't pass your anxiety to your kid. Children take their cues from their parents. They look to the parents for information about interpreting ambiguous situations. When your child witnesses you in an utter state of anxiety, it is unsettling for him. If your go-to response in a situation is to become scared, fearful, or anxious, your child will think such situations are unsafe. Despite your best intentions, you are unknowingly communicating your stress and anxiety to the kid. Not a lot of adults realize this, but children are quick learners and good observers. How you present yourself in a stressful situation will teach him his basic stress responses. If you are dealing with any anxiety, ensure that you don't feel guilty about it. Experiencing or living with anxiety is not easy. Understanding that it's not your fault and accepting the situation is the first step to tackle it.

The transmission of anxiety from a parent to a kid is inevitable. The second thing you need to do is ensure that you don't do this. So, you need to learn to manage your anxiety first. You cannot be of much help to your child while crumbling under pressure. By letting your emotions get the best of you, you are setting a poor example for him.

When you're struggling with your anxiety, keeping calm becomes difficult. You can also talk about what you are feeling when overwhelmed by your emotions. Learning stress management techniques according to your specific needs and requirements is helpful. When you learn to tolerate stress, you are showing your child how to cope with stressful situations or uncertainty and doubt. An important part of treating children with anxiety is to teach stress tolerance to parents. This is a simultaneous process that works in both directions. When you set a good example of how to manage stress, you are essentially showing your child how to stay calm.

The different stress management techniques you use can be used by your child whenever he feels anxious. For instance, thinking rationally becomes incredibly difficult during stressful times. A simple exercise you can use to concentrate on your breathing is something your child can also practice whenever he feels anxious. Another technique you can use is the rationalization of thoughts. If something is overwhelming or stressing you, communicate about it to your child. Once you state the problem, talk about scary situations and the likely outcome. Ask your child, how likely do you think the situation is bound to come true? Practicing realistic thinking is a great stress-relieving activity.

While dealing with a stressful situation, pay extra attention to your facial expressions and body language. Body language communicates more than words ever can. If your face looks tensed, scared, or worried, your child will pick on it. Learn to choose your words carefully, regulate the intensity of your emotions, and pay attention to your facial expressions. Your child is a sponge and he's picking up on everything you are saying and doing.

You might not want your child to see you during an anxious situation, but don't try to suppress your emotions. Avoiding any issue and emotion suppression are two things that you need to avoid at all costs. This teaches unhealthy and maladaptive coping mechanisms to your kid. Instead of suppressing what you are feeling, talk to your child about what is causing your anxiety. When he knows you're stressed and are working on reducing that stress or maintaining a positive outlook, it becomes easier for him to understand what to do. Seeing a parent cope with stress is okay and healthy for a child. At the same time, you should also explain why you chose to react the way you did.

For instance, let's say you lost your cool because you were worried about not getting your child to school on time. Once he is back home from school or when you feel calmer, talk to him about the stressful situation. Tell him you were quite anxious in the morning when he was getting late for school and you managed your anxiety by yelling. At the same time, also tell him that this was not an ideal reaction. Teach him better ways to cope with stress instead of yelling. You can set a good example by talking about anxiety. This gives your child the permission to express and feel his stress. Acknowledgment goes a long way in helping your child manage anxiety.

You cannot avoid stressful situations and circumstances in life. Regardless of how hard you try, stress is a part of life. So, you need to create a plan of action to deal with stressful situations and triggers. If you get stressed when deadlines are fast approaching or anxious if your child doesn't go to bed on time, talk to him about it. It's always better to have a reasonable conversation and create a plan of action that can be implemented instead of giving in to your emotions.

Learn to disengage. At times, prolonging a conversation does more harm than good. If you believe a specific situation is worsening the stress you are experiencing, disengage. For instance, if you are unable to deal with the anxiety of dropping your child at school, ask your partner, friend, or another family member to step in for you. Learning your limits is as important as working on overcoming your anxieties and fears. If you start giving in to your anxiety whenever you need to drop your child at school, it conveys the wrong message. Sooner or later, your child will form an unhealthy association that being dropped off at school or going to school is an act that upsets his parents. You don't want your child to have such unhealthy associations. So, become mindful of your reactions and responses to stress.

Whenever you start to feel a little overwhelmed in the presence of your child, permit yourself to take a break from it. For instance, if you're getting stressed about a work-related issue and your child is in the same room, step away from the room. Before you do this, tell him you need a break for five minutes and will be back within five minutes. By explaining what you are experiencing and what you plan to do, it gives him a better idea of what's expected of him. It also shows him better anxiety coping mechanisms.

Dear parents, you need a support system in place to help your anxiety too. You are your child's support system, so who is yours? Whether it is your spouse, partner, friends, family members, or colleagues at work, you need people to depend on in moments of extreme anxiety or stress. If not, you can join a support group, seek professional help, or anything else that calms you down. Learning to manage your anxiety can work wonders for a child's anxiety. Instead of fueling his fears and anxiety, manage your own. It is okay to take a break, it is okay to ask for help, and it is certainly okay to make time for yourself. Practicing a little self-care can work wonders for your health. You will learn more about self-care techniques in the next chapter.

CHAPTER FOURTEEN

Self -Care Tips for Parents

Once you are a parent, your life undergoes a major transformation. You have now entered a role that never really ends. Whether it is a young child, teenager, or adult, you never stop playing the role of a parent. Taking care of your child will always be a priority. As parents, we're all constantly worried about their health, finances, success, social life, and other achievements. Apart from this, we also worry about their overall happiness. All this is quite normal and it is a part of your job description.

You are a parent, but there are other roles you need to play too. Whether it is your professional or personal commitments, you need to manage those as well. As an adult, you will have your own set of worries. From finances to relationships, your job, health, and everything else, there is a lot to manage.

At times, all this becomes incredibly overwhelming. You probably realize all the different things your child worries about and steps you can use to promote their self-care. It is time to concentrate on selfcare. When there are so many obligations and responsibilities you need to juggle, self-care is the first thing that goes out of the window. A common reason why parents are constantly overwhelmed, tired, or even anxious is because they have no time to take care of themselves. In your attempt to take care of everyone in your life, you are compromising on yourself. Stop doing this.

Until now, the importance of being a mindful parent while dealing with an anxious child was repeatedly stressed. Well, it's not just children who need to be taken care of, but even you need to do this for yourself. Self-care is important. Taking care of your own needs ensures that you are your best self while dealing with your child. Parenting your anxious little one can be an all-consuming job. When you are constantly stressed and worried about him, it will sooner or later take a toll on you. This is one of the reasons why you need to prioritize your health and wellbeing too. Here are some simple suggestions you can use to practice self-care.

Start Prioritizing

You are a human being and not superhuman. Let go of the notion that you can do everything. The first step is to accept your human nature. It is okay to let go and not do everything. If you have multiple obligations, start prioritizing. Most of your priorities might involve your child, family members, and other loved ones. Take some time, find a quiet spot, and make a list of all your obligations and responsibilities. From this list, select one or two obligations that are the most important for you. For instance, you might like knitting, gardening, painting, or watching movies. Whatever it is, select two items from this list and prioritize them. If there's someone else in the house you can share your responsibilities with, divide your responsibilities.

Once you have your list of priorities, ensure that you concentrate on them. Don't compromise on self-care for the sake of everything else. Unless you are at your 100%, you cannot be of much help to anyone. Give yourself the permission to enjoy life and take care of yourself. It is okay to worry about your child, but your worries become more manageable and less overwhelming when you are physically, mentally, and emotionally refreshed.

Take Some Time Out

Yes, you have hundreds of responsibilities to manage. When there are so many duties that need to be performed, 24 hours might not seem sufficient. Remember the simple announcement on airplanes about putting on your oxygen mask first before helping others. You become better at taking care of others when you take care of yourself. The good thing about self-care is it doesn't have to be a chore that takes up hours together. 20 minutes daily for self-care will do. Whether it is 20 minutes to read, engaging in your hobbies, talking to someone, or taking a break, do whatever you want. You not only need a break but deserve it too. Plan your days such that you get some time for yourself. Don't feel guilty for taking time for self-care.

Spending Time With Your Loved Ones

A simple way to de-stress and let go of any unnecessary worries and feel better is by spending time with your loved ones. Humans have always thrived as groups. This is how civilizations were formed and societies created. We need others around us. We are not lone wolves. Whether it is your family, friends, or colleagues, spend some time with those who make you feel better. If you are swamped with taking care of your child, professional responsibilities, and personal obligations, you will become overwhelmed. If you believe you don't have as much time as you used to initially to go out and meet your friends, set up weekly phone calls. Set a day aside from your daily routines to spend time with those you love. You will feel better.

Schedule Fun Activities

Make a note of all the diff erent activities you love and enjoy. Once you have this list ready, it's time to schedule some fun into your daily routine. Yes, you read it right. You need to schedule fun activities. It might sound contradictory that you need to plan for fun, but it works. There are several things you might enjoy. At times, even going over the list of diff erent activities you enjoy tends to become stressful. After all, there are 24 hours per day at your disposal. If there are multiple things you want to do, you need to make time for it by planning. For instance, you might like reading, doing yoga, watching TV, baking, or even going for a leisurely walk. Why don't you plan your day such that you can include at least one of these activities daily? This is more doable than getting stressed looking at the list. At least this way you are doing something that you like.

Pamper Yourself

Dear parent, your child is not the only one that needs to be pampered. All children expect to be pampered. Whether it is staying up late to watch a movie or going out for occasional ice cream, these are all treats kids enjoy. Well, now it's time to do the same thing for yourself. Once in a while, pamper yourself. Whether it is getting a manicure-pedicure, going on a shopping spree, or even treating yourself to ice cream, do it. You need an occasional treat too. You deserve that!

Go Out

Getting out of the house shouldn't be synonymous with running errands, going to the grocery store, or dropping off laundry. You need to go out of the house and kitchen. Whether it is going for a walk or a long drive, spend some time outside the house. Don't restrict yourself to work or the house

alone. Take a break to cool off. Heading outdoors helps break free of the confinements of daily life. Have a parent night out once a week or maybe every alternate week. If you schedule this into your daily routine, it becomes easier. Even your children will become more accommodating and understanding of your time to cool off. If you know you have to go out once a month, you can make alternate arrangements to take care of your kids. It will also give you something to look forward to. Do you count the days until you can go on a holiday or a vacation? Why do you do this? Because it gives you something to look forward to! Well, why don't you give yourself something to look forward to by scheduling some time off your usual parental responsibilities?

Organization Matters

A simple way to take care of yourself is by creating a schedule. When you stay on top of all your responsibilities and obligations, the stress associated with them melts away. For instance, if you're worried about your finances, spend some time and create a plan of action that helps restabilize your financial situation. Instead of worrying about it, you are doing something to tackle the stress. In all conversations about self-care, the importance of organizing is always emphasized. If your professional or personal life is in disarray, any stress you experience increases. If managing the necessities of daily life itself becomes stressful, you cannot find the time to relax. Whether you are using a to-do list, doing meal prep, or organizing your closet, find an efficient way to bring some order into your life. When there is order, chaos goes away. The lack of chaos automatically eliminates stress. Why worry about tackling stress if you can prevent it from cropping up altogether?

Concentrate On Your Future

When all your time and energy goes toward taking care of your children, planning for the future, and securing it, you might not have any time to think about yourself. This is one common mistake most parents make. We get so caught up in our responsibilities we forget to plan for our future. As your child grows, he will become more independent. It means you will have more time for yourself. The best way to ensure your future is something you desire by planning for it. It means you need to think about your lifestyle, career changes (if any), and your dreams. Start saving for your future. Whether it is retirement or a world trip, you need to concentrate on saving for it too. Planning and preparation are important.

Your Health is Important

Never ignore your health for the sake of others. You need to take care of your physical, mental, and emotional wellbeing. Whether it is an anxious child at home or any other common cause of worry, your health needs to be a priority too. Don't skip your doctor's appointments! Concentrate on getting sufficient sleep at night, consuming a healthy diet, and exercising regularly. When you practice healthy lifestyle habits, you are setting a good example for your kid to follow. After all, most of the behaviors children pick up are from the adults around. So, why don't you start modeling some good behavior?

For instance, how do you respond to stress? If your answer is to get overwhelmed, have an emotional outburst, or do something along these lines, you are setting a poor example. If you want your child to manage stress, you need to set a good example.

Always remember, practice before you preach.

By following the simple and practical tips given in this chapter, you can ensure that self-care becomes a priority too. Let go of any guilt associated with spending time for yourself. You deserve it too.

CONCLUSION

We all have our own set of worries and insecurities. Whether it is an adult or a young child, fears, insecurities, and worries are common. Children are trying to make sense of the world around them. They slowly understand the relationship between cause and effect. Childhood fears are incredibly common. Whether it is the fear of the boogeyman or the dark, your child will be afraid of one thing or the other. By now, you might have realized how common anxiety is these days. Children and adults alike suffer from anxiety caused by different reasons. From biological factors to environmental conditioning and atmosphere at home, different factors can cause childhood anxiety. This anxiety can present itself as social anxiety, panic attacks, excessive worry or fear, or even separation anxiety. The first step towards tackling all this is to understand what causes these anxieties and what triggers them.

In this book, you were introduced to what anxiety means, how it influences the brain, chemical imbalances that result in anxiety, and signs and symptoms to watch out for. Even though fears are common, when these fears prevent your child from living his life to the fullest, they become problematic. Apart from considering regular treatment options for anxiety such as cognitive behavioral therapy or any other form of therapy, there are different things you can do to help alleviate his anxiety. One thing you're never supposed to do is swoop in and try to fix things. Ignore the parental instinct of trying to save the day for your child. The best thing you can do is teach him to manage his anxiety and regulate his thoughts. This is a great way to raise an independent and confident child. These valuable skills you equip him will stay with him all life long.

Parenting is a full-time job without any breaks or vacations. Whether it is a toddler or a teenager, you never stop being a parent. Worrying about your child's overall wellbeing is a part of a parent's job description. So, it is time for you to take corrective action and guide your child in the right direction. Several things cannot be regulated or even predicted in life. The good news is, anxiety can be managed and eliminated. It will take consistent effort, patience, conscious changes, and resilience, but your efforts will be worth it.

Knowingly or unknowingly, most parents feed their child's fears. They might also encourage their child to fuel his fears. These are two things you need to avoid. In this book, you were introduced to a list of desirable and undesirable responses you need to avoid while dealing with an anxious child. Instead, a favorable approach is to teach your child to manage, face, and overcome his fears. Whether you are using the stepladder approach or are reworking the negative associations with positive ones, there are different techniques you can use. Depending on your child and his temperament, choose one that works well for you.

Another tip all parents need to remember is to never force their child to do anything he isn't ready for. Even a seemingly simple activity might seem frightening to your child. Do not dismiss his worries and anxieties. Instead, acknowledge and validate his feelings. Start a healthy and honest conversation about anxiety. The thing about fears is, they lose their power once you start talking about them. Encourage your child to be forthcoming about his worries. It is your responsibility to ensure that your child can reach out to you in times of his need.

In this book, you were given all the information required to recognize the progress your child makes while preventing the chances of relapses, identifying his triggers and fears, and helping your child think realistically. By equipping him with the skills required to face the fear and fight, you are teaching him to plan for a better future. You are not alone in this situation. Dealing with your child's anxieties is not easy, but it is doable. Before you work on helping your child elevate his anxieties, ensure that you have all the information required. This is where this book steps into the picture. It will act as your guide every step of the way. Whenever in doubt, refer to the information and simple suggestions given in this book. It's not just your child's help that is important, concentrate on yourself too. Dear parent, you cannot be of much help to the child unless you are functioning effectively and efficiently. Follow the simple self-care suggestions given in this book and you will see a positive change.

While you implement these suggestions about tackling your child's fears or anxiety, ensure that you consider his comfort level too. All children are unique. So, what might work for one might not necessarily work for your kid. Don't get discouraged or disheartened. If something isn't working, try another route! There is no scientific guide to parenting. It is a process of trial and error. Don't mistake your child's introversion for anxiety. Understanding his personality, temperament, and development is important. If you push your child to do something he isn't ready for yet, it will backfire. You need to be his support system, pillar of strength, and cheerleader. Regulate your emotions, thoughts, and feelings before concentrating on your little one.

I understand the difficulties and tricky aspects of parenting an anxious child. All the suggestions discussed in this book are based on my personal experience. Through years of research and implementation, I have seen a positive change in my little one. I know he is shaping up to be a confident and independent teenager. Don't worry too much because I've got your back. Don't hesitate to reach out to your loved ones in the time of need. You don't have to go through this alone!

Now that you are equipped with all the information you need, it is time to implement the simple and practical suggestions and tips discussed in this book. One important thing you need to remember while implementing these suggestions is to be incredibly patient. Never lose your patience and stay calm and composed even when your child is anxious. After all, he's counting on you for strength and support during his anxious times. It will take a consistent and conscious effort to equip your little one with the skills and tools required to tackle anxiety. Helping your child lead an anxiety-free life is possible. Take the first step towards this goal and get started immediately.

Finally, if you have enjoyed reading this book and found it informative, take a couple of minutes and leave a review on Amazon! Your feedback can help several other parents who are in the same situation as you.

Thank you and all the best!

REFERENCES

All images sourced from Pixabay.

6 major types of anxiety disorders. (2019, July 10). CHOC Children's Blog.

https://blog.chocchildrens.org/6-major-typesof-anxiety-disorders/

8 Myths About Anxiety in Children and Teens. (2019, July 7).

Goodbye Anxiety, Hello Joy.

https://goodbyeanxietyhellojoy. com/myths-about-anxiety/

10 Self-Care Tips for Parents. (2020, January 8). MGH Clay Center for Young Healthy Minds.

https://www.mghclaycenter. org/parenting-concerns/10-self-care-tips-for-parents/

Anderson, E., & Shivakumar, G. (2013). Effects of Exercise and Physical Activity on Anxiety. Frontiers in Psychiatry, 4.

https:// doi.org/10.3389/fpsyt.2013.00027

Anxiety disorders Symptoms & Causes | Boston Children's Hospital. (n.d.). Www.childrens hospital.org.

https://www. childrenshospital.org/conditions-and-treatments/conditions/a/ anxiety-disorders/symptoms-and-causes

Childhood fears: What's common and how can you help? - Children's Health. (2019). Childrens.com.

https://www. childrens.com/health-wellness/childhood-fears

Cullens, A. (2017). 7 Effective Ways to Help Children Overcome Social Anxiety. Big Life Journal.

https://biglifejournal.com/ blogs/blog/help-children-overcome-social-anxiety-failure

Data and Statistics on Children's Mental Health. (2019, April 19). Centers for Disease Control and Prevention.

https://www.cdc.gov/childrensmentalhealth/data.html#ref

Data and Statistics on Children's Mental Health | CDC. (2020, June 15). Centers for Disease Control and Prevention.

https://www.cdc.gov/childrensmentalhealth/data.html#:~:text=7.4%25%20of%20children%20aged%203

Davies, M. N., Verdi, S., Burri, A., Trzaskowski, M., Lee, M., Hettema, J. M., Jansen, R., Boomsma, D. I., & Spector, T. D. (2015). Generalised Anxiety Disorder – A Twin Study of Genetic Architecture, Genome-Wide Association and Differential Gene Expression. PLOS ONE, 10(8), e0134865.

https://doi.org/10.1371/journal.pone.0134865

Don't Argue With a Brain Glitch. (10 Do's and 5 Don'ts for Parents of Kids with OCD). (n.d.). OCD • Anxiety • Psychologists • Psychotherapists • Ontario.

https://www.turningpointpsychology.ca/blog/children-with-ocd-guidelinesfor-parents

Eapen, V. (2014). Developmental and mental health disorders: Two sides of the same coin. Asian Journal of Psychiatry, 8, 7–11.

https://doi.org/10.1016/j.ajp.2013.10.007

Ehmke, R. (2016, March 10). Helping Children Cope After a Traumatic Event. Child Mind Institute; Child Mind Institute.

https://childmind.org/guide/helping-children-cope-traumaticevent/

Ferguson, S. (2019, June 27). Is Anxiety Genetic? Healthline; Healthline Media.

https://www.healthline.com/health/mentalhealth/is-anxiety-genetic#symptoms

Ghandour, R. M., Sherman, L. J., Vladutiu, C. J., Ali, M. M., Lynch, S. E., Bitsko, R. H., & Blumberg, S. J. (2019). Prevalence and Treatment of Depression, Anxiety, and Conduct Problems in US Children. The Journal of Pediatrics, 206, 256-267.e3.

https://doi.org/10.1016/j.jpeds.2018.09.021

Gomstyn, A. (n.d.). Kids and anxiety: What's normal, what's not. Aetna.

https://www.aetna.com/health-guide/kids-anxietywhats-normal-seek-help.html

Gottschalk, M. G., & Domschke, K. (2016). Novel developments in genetic and epigenetic mechanisms of anxiety. Current Opinion in Psychiatry, 29(1), 32–38.

https://doi.org/10.1097/yco.0000000000000219

Gottschalk, M. G., & Domschke, K. (2017). Genetics of generalized anxiety disorder and related traits. Dialogues in Clinical Neuroscience, 19(2), 159–168.

https://www.ncbi.nlm.nih.gov/pmc/articles/PMC5573560/

How to Ease Your Child's Separation Anxiety. (2019).

HealthyChildren.org.
https://www.healthychildren.org/

English/ages-stages/toddler/Pages/Soothing-Your-ChildsSeparation-Anxiety.aspx

Hurley, K. (2016). 10 Things Never to Say to Your Anxious Child - Pyscom.net. Psycom.net - Mental Health Treatment Resource since 1986.

https://www.psycom.net/child-anxietythings-never-to-say

Hurley, K. (2016). Helping Kids with Anxiety: Strategies to Help Anxious Children. Psycom.net - Mental Health Treatment Resource since 1986.

https://www.psycom.net/help-kids-withanxiety

Kelly, K. (2019, August 6). 8 Self-Soothing Techniques for Your Young Child. Understood.org; Understood.

https://www. understood.org/en/friends-feelings/managing-feelings/fear/8self-soothing-techniques-for-your-young-child

Morris-Rosendahl, D. J. (2002). Are there anxious genes? Dialogues in Clinical Neuroscience, 4(3), 251–260.

https://www.ncbi.nlm.nih.gov/pmc/articles/PMC3181683/

Panic attacks in children - tips for parents on how to help your child cope. (n.d.). Priory Group.

https://www.priorygroup. com/blog/panic-attacks-in-children-tips-for-parents-on-howto-help-your-child-cope

Perciavalle, V., Blandini, M., Fecarotta, P., Buscemi, A., Di Corrado, D., Bertolo, L., Fichera, F., &

Coco, M. (2017). The role of deep breathing on stress. Neurological Sciences : Official Journal of the Italian Neurological Society and of the Italian Society of Clinical Neurophysiology, 38(3), 451–458

https:// doi.org/10.1007/s10072-016-2790-8

Qin, S., Young, C. B., Duan, X., Chen, T., Supekar, K., & Menon, V. (2014). Amygdala Subregional Structure and Intrinsic Functional Connectivity Predicts Individual Differences in Anxiety During Early Childhood. Biological Psychiatry, 75(11), 892–900.

https://doi.org/10.1016/j.biopsych.2013.10.006

Reeb-Sutherland, B. C. (2017). What Environmental Factors Contribute to the Development of Anxiety in Temperamentally Inhibited Children? Insight From Animal Research Models. Policy Insights from the Behavioral and Brain Sciences, 5(1), 126–133.

https://doi.org/10.1177/2372732217743990

Schatz Beck, D, & Rostain, A. L. (2006). ADHD With Comorbid Anxiety. Journal of Attention Disorders, 10(2), 141–149.

https://doi.org/10.1177/1087054706286698

Smith, K. (2016). 6 Types of Anxiety that Can Affect Children and How to Help. Psycom.net - Mental Health Treatment Resource since 1986.

https://www.psycom.net/6-types-anxietyand-kids

Talking to Your Child or Teen About Anxiety | Here to Help. (n.d.). Www.heretohelp.bc.ca.

https://www.heretohelp.bc.ca/infosheet/talking-to-your-child-or-teen-aboutanxiety#:~:text=When%20your%20child%20expresses%20 anxiety

Thoma, M. V., La Marca, R., Brönnimann, R., Finkel, L., Ehlert, U., & Nater, U. M. (2013). The Effect of Music on the Human Stress Response. PLoS ONE, 8(8), e70156.

https://doi. org/10.1371/journal.pone.0070156

Treatment | Anxiety and Depression Association of America, ADAA. (2019). Adaa.org.

https://adaa.org/living-with-anxiety/children/treatment

Types of Developmental Delays in Children. (2019). Nyulangone.org.

https://nyulangone.org/conditions/
developmental-delays-in-children/types

Walters Wright, L. (2019, October 16). Signs of Anxiety in Young Kids. Understood.org; Understood.

https://www.understood. org/en/friends-feelings/managing-feelings/stress-anxiety/signsyour-young-child-might-be-struggling-with-anxiety

What Can Cause a Relapse of Child Anxiety? (2016, February 28). Turnaroundanxiety.com.

https://www.turnaroundanxiety. com/hey-boys-im-baaaack-what-to-do-when-anxiety-returns/

Young, K. (2016, May 11). Phobias and Fears in Children - Powerful Strategies To Try. Hey Sigmund.

https://www. heysigmund.com/phobias-and-fears-in-children/

Zargarzadeh, M., & Shirazi, M. (2014). The effect of progressive muscle relaxation method on test anxiety in nursing students. Iranian Journal of Nursing and Midwifery Research, 19(6),607–612.

https://www.ncbi.nlm.nih.gov/pmc/articles/ PMC4280725/

BOOK 2

Helping Your Anxious Teen

A Practical Guide for Parents To Help Your
Child Learn To Manage Everyday Anxiety

INTRODUCTION

Anxiety in teens and tweens is rapidly increasing with time. It is believed that one in fiveteenagers is highly likely to suffer from chronic anxiety once during their young age. Despite being well-informed and well-aware, some parents may still fail to decipher the real issue and help their kids cope.

Has your teen been complaining about consistent stomach aches or any other health issues? Are they constantly afraid of attending school or public places? Do you notice perpetual mood swings in your teen?

Instead of rolling your eyes and thinking to yourself, "Here we go again," try to dig deeper as the issue may be more serious than you think. Start by comforting them by helping them to find solutions to solve the issues immediately. However, if they fail to budge or cooperate, you might get impatient, but that this will only make the situation worse for your teen. They are already feeling irked and frustrated, so you don't want to add to their existing discontentment.

If you wish to ease your child's agony, you must learn about the real issue and look for signs related to anxiety. Teens are already going through a lot in their adolescent years due to rising competition, peer pressure, and hormonal changes. It can worsen their anxiety and make the situation entirely threatening.

Since anxiety can harm your teen's physical, mental, and emotional health, it is necessary to recognize the signs early. Some may even show poor performance at school, affecting their chances of getting into a good university or excelling at their career as they grow up. Treating chronic anxiety is very important as it can abate the chances of suicidal ideas and selfharm.

This book is packed with all the information needed to recognize and delve deeper into the issue of anxiety and related disorders. Since this subject can be complicated and sensitive, pay attention to every aspect this book illustrates as it is bound to help every anxiety-related issue. Having been through similar problems related to teens, chronic anxiety, and related issues, this book provides practical insights since it is based on factual information and real-life experiences.

If you can relate to these factors, take your child's condition seriously without waiting to recognize further relevance. With time, failing to treat chronic anxiety can be life-threatening and cause irreversible damage. While teens struggle to control their feelings and lash out easily compared to adults, their treatment can be more effective as their fury is often related to a cry for help.

If you have been feeling similar angst and need to take the necessary steps to help your teen cope with the torment of anxiety, this book will teach you the right way to approach this issue. It has everything you need to know, from learning about the signs to seeking help in extreme situations. As parents, you will also learn some self-care tips and ways to treat your own issues to help your child overcome theirs. Read on to begin the journey toward healing your teen's anxiety.

CHAPTER 1

UNDERSTANDING ANXIETY

The first step to cure any anxiety issue is un derstanding it in depth. At times, anxiety is disregarded as merely a mental "mood" that comes and goes. It is necessary for guardians and parents to understand anxiety's real meaning and dig deeper to decipher the crux of the issue. Since anxiety is often deep-rooted, it can be a bit difficult to treat. However, it's not impossible. To effectively treat this mental health issue means learning about what anxiety is and the causes that may have triggered it.

What is Anxiety?

Anxiety is created by your body when it prepares you to face threats around you. In other words, your body tries to keep you safe in dangerous situations and motivates you to fight them. Let's say that you are walking on the road, tired after a long day at work and wanting to get into bed and rest. However, your lethargy and laziness instantly pass once you encounter any danger around you. For example, you spot a snake on the road, your body will instantly increase its energy levels and compel you to run, despite being tired. Even though random bursts of anxiety can be helpful, regularly facing this issue can affect your health and lifestyle in the long run. For example, new beginnings, such as moving or starting a new job, can make a person anxious. However, this anxious feeling can boost confidence and help a person perform better. Your body's reaction to something that is not an actual or obvious threat or challenge can trigger this mental health issue.

Anxiety is often confused with getting worried. Even though every individual is prone to feeling worried and nervous in certain situations, not everyone is necessarily an anxiety patient. In some cases, anxiety

is often misunderstood by most people and treated like another temporary health issue. In reality, this mental health problem can degrade a person's quality of life and push them into a downward spiral if left untreated for a prolonged period. In extreme cases, anxiety can trigger serious health issues debilitating your life. As mentioned, it can be effectively treated once you learn more about the origins.

What Causes Anxiety?

While normal or ordinary anxiety is a feeling commonly experienced by just about everyone, it can become a major issue if you keep feeling worried and fear the consequences all the time. Several aspects can result in anxiety, namely-

1. Genetics

Individuals with a family history of anxiety or other mental health issues are highly likely to experience anxiety. Even though they may have had a happy childhood, witnessing their parents undergoing anxiety can also have a major impact on their mental health.

2. Physical Health Conditions

People with certain physical health conditions, such as epilepsy, asthma, diabetes, and certain allergies, are more prone to developing anxiety. In turn, this can affect and worsen their physical health and make treatment difficult. However, being anxious and undergoing physical health issues can help your medical practitioner diagnose the issue easily.

3. Personality Traits

If you have inherited or developed certain personality traits growing up, you may develop anxiety. For example, being extremely shy or a perfectionist are some traits that may lead to anxiety disorders. However, not every individual with distinct traits is susceptible to developing anxiety.

4. Traumatic Experiences

If a person has undergone an extremely traumatic experience and finds it difficult to deal with past emotions, they may develop PTSD, which is a form of anxiety disorder. It can also occur due to stressful events that are too difficult to overcome. Some examples of such stressful events include emotional or physical abuse, pregnancy, personal or professional problems, or the demise of a loved one.

While these are the known reasons that trigger anxiety, several studies and research are ongoing to decipher the exact reason.

Types of Anxiety Disorders

Anxiety disorders are emotional issues triggered by extreme worrying, feelings of fear, and staying anxious most of the time. While women are more prone to suffer from an anxiety disorder, men should also be mindful of this emotional issue.

Let's take a look at some common types of anxiety disorders that many teenagers and young adults face.

1. Panic Disorder

When your anxiety reaches a peak level, your body may respond by triggering symptoms like heavy breathing, fast heart rate, cold or hot flashes, nausea, and excessive sweating. These signs indicate that a person is experiencing a panic attack and should be treated by a mental health practitioner. Since panic attacks can occur anytime and anywhere, especially during intense situations, this disorder should be treated at the earliest. While some individuals experience just one panic attack in their lifetime, others may face recurring episodes that can worsen their situation and lifestyle.

2. Social Anxiety Disorder

This disorder is entrenched in the fear of being judged and not being "good enough" for others. It can lead to feelings of awkwardness and discomfort in social settings. Commonly known as social phobia, this disorder makes individuals avoid attending social events and keeps them isolated. The constant fear of doing something embarrassing and judgmental stares makes them shy or nervous. To alleviate such situations, they avoid going to new places and meeting people altogether. Occurrences like meeting an old friend at the grocery store and making small talk are also difficult for them.

3. Generalized Anxiety Disorder

This disorder is an emotional disorder where the person undergoes excessive worrying and feels burdened all the time. Individuals with generalized anxiety disorder often loathe themselves because they keep worrying about meager things, even about how they worry over such insignificant factors. Teenagers are more prone to this disorder due to the unwanted pressure they face daily. The inability to control the amount of worrying they do is also a sign of this disorder. Due to this, they are often unable to sleep or focus on their work.

4. Obsessive-Compulsive Disorder

Commonly known as OCD, this anxiety disorder puts the patient in a circuit of trundling certain actions. Their obsessive behavior can lead to anxious thoughts, which, in turn, increases panic. For example, placing certain items in an aligned way or feeling restless until certain things are organized are common signs and behavioral aspects of OCD. With time, this anxiety disorder results in the person performing repeated actions and developing irrational thoughts. Simple actions like going back and forth to check and double-check if they have locked the door or organizing their drawer in the order of specific colors are some examples of repeated behaviors in OCD.

5. Agoraphobia

Agoraphobia is the fear of experiencing a panic attack in a place where they might not receive any help. It keeps the person from attending social events or public places for long periods. They also prefer to keep away from crowds and long queues. This disorder can worsen if the person visits a place where they have experienced a panic attack before. Individuals who have Agoraphobia need someone to accompany them when waiting in queues or catching a bus. They may also feel more anxious when they cannot leave certain places at will.

While these five anxiety disorders are the most common, some may even experience other types such as separation anxiety disorder, post-traumatic stress disorder (PTSD), illness anxiety disorder, and certain phobias.

Common Signs of Anxiety

Feeling on Edge or Nervous Most of the Time

If you or your loved one feels nervous or worried regularly, consider it a sign of anxiety. At times, feeling nervous about the smallest or ludicrous things is a common sign in individuals with anxiety. Due to this, they fear going out in public spaces or meeting new people. You might have noticed that people with anxiety lack socializing skills because meeting new people and starting conversations makes them anxious. Their habit of obsessive thinking and impending panic can thereby affect their lifestyle quality.

Facing Difficulty Concentrating

Your mind is constantly thinking about the downside and focusing on the negative aspects of the situation, diverting your attention and diminishing your concentration levels. Turning an incoming piece of information into a cohesive fact becomes even more difficult when you have anxiety, thereby affecting your ability to focus and complete even simple duties. This, in turn, results in delayed tasks and pushes your goals further away. Real-time reasoning is a sign of a healthy brain, but it can be affected by recurring thoughts related to fear and worry. In turn, your brain shifts focus to insignificant aspects.

Feeling Overwhelmed

The inability to concentrate also adds to an overwhelming feeling, which can further worsen the condition. Irrespective of the task you are supposed to complete, the overwhelming feeling keeps you restrained and does not allow you to accomplish the simplest tasks. This feeling also veils the real trigger that provoked the negative emotion, which is why individuals often confuse it with anger. The stress hormone cortisol is released by your body when you feel worried and overwhelmed, as this can lead to extreme anxiety and worsen the situation. Equally, the hormone responsible for fighting anxiety is also reduced.

Constantly Worrying About Things Going Bad

Even if the situation is in their favor, people who have anxiety find it difficult to look at the positive side. Instead, they focus on the negative aspects and worry about things going wrong even if there is no such possibility of it happening. In the long run, such individuals will face trouble sleeping, causing other issues like insomnia. With time, the person may turn into a pessimist and fail to acknowledge any situation's positive side affecting their personal and professional life.

Heavy Breathing and Heart Palpitations

In some cases, individuals may show physical signs during anxiety attacks, such as heavy breathing, adrenaline rush, a boost in energy level, stomach twisting, and heart palpitations. Some people even face extreme sweating and shaking. As mentioned, these signs are related to the advent of panic attacks that can turn into recurring episodes if left untreated. Panic attacks are often confused with anxiety attacks as they share similar signs. If you or your loved ones experience an anxiety or panic attack, consult a medical practitioner as soon as you can.

Even though these are the most common signs and symptoms of anxiety, they can vary from person to person. Monitor the behavior and signs to diagnose their anxiety disorder. It will also help you get optimum treatment for the specific condition.

Difference Between Anxiety and Fear

Most misinformed people confuse anxiety with fear, and these are used interchangeably. In reality, fear is a negative emotion triggered due to a known cause or situation. On the other hand, the real reason behind anxiety is often unknown or shrouded. Since both emotions lead to a stressful outcome, individuals get confused between anxiety and fear. The most common physiological signs and symptoms of both anxiety and fear are increased heart rate, sweating, muscle tension, and some may even experience shortness of breath.

While fear often leads to a negative occurrence due to the visibility of danger, anxiety is only limited to the possibility of experiencing something negative or dangerous. In other words, fear is related to an immediate threat, whereas anxiety is related to the prospects of finding yourself in a dangerous situation.

Key Takeaway: Anxiety is a common feeling that most people experience on a day-to-day basis. While it helps you overcome unwanted situations, recurring anxiety should be treated as it can ruin a person's health and lifestyle. Physical and emotional health issues, trauma, genetics, and environmental conditions are some common reasons for anxiety. It is imperative to learn about the various anxiety disorder types to diagnose and treat patients effectively. Furthermore, it's important to comprehend the common signs of anxiety to help yourself or your loved one.

CHAPTER 2

TEENS AND ANXIETY

It's very common for teenagers to suffer from anx iety or anxiety disorders. Teenagers are more prone to develop anxiety because teenage years are the time to try new experiences, face new challenges, and take new opportunities. It's also the time when their brains start changing, and they seek more independence. Simple stages like secondary school, college, fitting in with other peers, and looking a certain way may be worrisome and stressful for a normal teenager. Additional to the responsibilities that fall on their shoulders at this age, they are pressured to become independent, like getting a job and living independently, making anxiety very common for teenagers. Especially since various adult emotions start developing during this period, this can cause anxiety to be common at this age. Although feelings of anxiousness do not last for most teenagers and tend to go away on their own, some teens struggle with persistent anxiety that becomes very intense, preventing them from participating in everyday activities. In this chapter, we discuss the struggles of teenagers with anxiety. What are the hidden anxiety signs? How can you interject and help your child with their difficult yet, completely normal mental condition?

Is Teenage Anxiety Normal?

This question becomes more and more persistent since you're spending a lot of time at home with your teens during quarantine. Eventually, this leads you to start questioning behaviors that you may have never seen from your teens before. The lack of physical contact with friends makes it even harder for your teenager to navigate normal social dynamics. Even their bodies will experience several changes due to the lack of privacy and reduced physical activity, not to mention how overwhelming it might be for your son or daughter to meet your expectations where learning and teaching experience technical changes.

All these factors make it normal for most teenagers to suffer from anxiety.

Anxiety Is Both Normal and Helpful

Anxiety is not only a normal physical response, but it is also helpful and puts your body into an alert state to prepare you for avoiding predator attacks. If you think about it, we all experience anxious emotions as we grow up. It's just that adults are more skilled in recognizing these emotions or physical signs. Nowadays, anxiety is much needed for many modern occasions that require you to perform at your best. For example, those butterflies you feel in your stomach before a presentation alert you to be adequately prepared. Normally, most of us experience anxiety before important events, but it's also normal for teenagers to experience slightly higher levels of anxious feelings, especially in situations where they feel like their future plans are not certain.

When Does Teenage Anxiety Become Intrusive?

Anxiety is a cause of concern when it starts limiting your teenager's function and affecting many areas of their life. Your teen may have an anxiety disorder if they tend to show exaggerated reactions to simple threats and complications. For example, starting college or high school may be a difficult and nerveracking experience for many young adults. However, a teenager with an anxiety disorder may even cease to function due to stress. They may emotionally and verbally shut down during classes. Some kids with severe anxiety may even attempt to avoid school. This is what health professionals would call an Anxiety Disorder. They use this term to refer to several conditions, including agoraphobia, separation anxiety disorder, social anxiety, panic disorder, selective mutism, and generalized anxiety disorder. At this point, these conditions may cause many parents to worry. However, it's important to stay reminded that anxiety is common among teenagers and can be treated easily.

The Difference Between Normal Anxiety and an Anxiety Disorder

It would be ideal for parents to be able to tell the difference between acceptable anxiety levels and intrusive ones so that they know when they should contact a mental health professional. As a parent, it is your priority to adjust to your child's behavior and accommodate their anxiety. You can tell if your teenager has an anxiety disorder by checking if they're quitting or avoiding daily routines or constantly complaining about unexplained fatigue, headaches, or stomachaches. A teenager with an anxiety disorder will also have impacted sleeping habits, school attendance, personal hygiene, or a drop in their school grades. Typically, you'll notice your teen becoming more sensitive or emotional or even defensive more often.

What Medications Can a 15 Year-Old Take for Anxiety?

1. Serotonin-Norepinephrine Reuptake Inhibitors or SNRIs

SNRIs contain a chemical substance that increases serotonin and norepinephrine and prevents the brain from reabsorbing them again at the same time. They can take up to a few weeks to show their full effects and may lead to similar side effects to another category of anxiety medications called Selective Serotonin Reuptake Inhibitors (SSRIs). Your child's doctor will check for potential side effects from both medications before choosing between SNRIs and SSRIs. The doctor will also consider things like your family history regarding how these medications have been received and the potential interactional effect with any other medications your teen takes.

2. Selective Serotonin Reuptake Inhibitors or SSRIs

SSRIs were initially antidepressants that improved mood by inhibiting the reuptake of the serotonin transmitter. They are the most com-mon type and usually the first type of medication prescribed to teenagers who have anxiety disorders. Their side effects, similar to SNRIs, include headaches, nausea, and sleeping problems. These side effects can take weeks to ease up, but it's important to ensure your teen does not quit their medication without consulting the doctor because sudden or premature discontinuation of many medications, especially antidepressants, can lead to uncomfortable withdrawal symptoms or flu-like symptoms.

3. Tricyclic Antidepressants or TCAs

Tricyclic antidepressants are usually prescribed when SNRIs and SSRIs are unhelpful. Your child's doctor may recommend an FDA-approved medication called clomipramine. Clomipramine soothes obsessivecompulsive disorder and social anxiety. However, TCAs pose a risk of serious side effects, such as sedation, constipation, and cardiac abnormalities. Therefore, patients who are prescribed TCAs are usually provided with regular EKGs to monitor their cardiac health. Your child's doctor must inform you about all the potential side effects and whether switching to TCAs is the best available option or not.

4. Benzodiazepines

It's not common for mental health doctors to prescribe benzodiazepines as a first treatment for a teenager with anxiety. These drugs can cause patients to develop a tolerance and become addicted to their medication. So, what are benzodiazepines? They are common sedating and anxiety medications that you've probably heard of before. These include Diazepam or Valium, alprazolam or Xanax, lorazepam or Ativan, and clonazepam or Klonopin. Incorrect discontinuation of any of these drugs can lead your teen to develop serious withdrawal symptoms. Most of the time, these drugs are prescribed along with SSRIs or SNRIs until the inhibitors reach their full effect.

What Are Signs of Anxiety in a Teenager?

The most obvious emotional signs of anxiety include irritability, restlessness, feeling on edge, difficulty concentrating, panic attacks, and unexplained outbursts. Here are other signs you may notice in a teenager with an anxiety disorder.

Physical Signs

Most of the anxiety's physical complaints can mimic the physical complaints of any average teen. However, the signs keep increasing as the person grows if they assuredly have an anxiety disorder. For example, headaches. While this might sound like a regular health complaint, frequent headaches are a cause of concern and may indicate that your teen has anxiety. Other common physical complaints include constant fatigue, gastrointestinal problems, not feeling well for no obvious medical cause, unexplained aches, and changing eating habits. Pay attention to any of these signs and follow up with a mental health professional if you notice any repetitive patterns.

Social Changes

Anxiety can be detected much easier by monitoring your teen's social interactions and activities because an anxiety disorder can significantly affect your child's relationships with their friends. A vital sign is if your teen was once a social person but gradually lost interest in their favorite activities or declined plans with their friends. It should also be obvious if they keep avoiding extracurricular activities and social interactions with their usual friends. Other signs include isolation from peer groups and spending a lot of time on their own.

Bad Performance at School

Anxiety can have a serious impact on your teen's performance at school. A teenager with an anxiety disorder would typically have disturbed sleeping patterns and eating habits, in addition to constantly missing school due to various physical issues they face dealing with everyday anxiety. It is very predictable for teenagers with untreated anxiety disorders to have poor academic performance. School workload can become very overwhelming for your teen with all their missed days and school avoidance thanks to their anxietyrelated illness and persistent worry. It may help you as a parent to look for signs like frequently missed assignments, complaints about overwhelming workload, negative jumps in grades, procrastination, and difficulty concentrating.

How Can I Help My Teenager with Anxiety?

A teenager who has an anxiety disorder may not be able to feel better on their own. This is why it's your duty as a parent to accommodate their anxiety and help them feel more comfortable at home. However, most parents are not educated enough to deal with constant stress, nervousness, and tension. Here is how you can be there for your teenager as they struggle with their daily anxiety symptoms.

Help Them Relax More

Achieving relaxation is not as simple as most people think. For example, you're not helping your teen relax by letting them chill in front of the TV or their computer screen. This can be even more stressful for them, depending on what they are watching. Tobacco, alcohol, and drugs may have the same impact on a person with anxiety - they provide a false, temporary state of relaxation. Naturally, what their bodies need is daily relaxation or breathing techniques that have a physical effect on their brain, and this can be achieved by practicing yoga, meditation, or even tai chi.

Make Sure They Are Connecting with Others

Hanging out or participating in organized activities with friends and family can be very effective in deepening your teenager's bonds with the people they feel the closest to. It will eventually make them feel more secure and supported, which can ease their symptoms. Plus, the fun and sharing in the whole experience of connecting with others will elevate their mood and increase their serotonin levels. Talking with someone who cares and listens to them will help them cope with their stress and feel more understood. If you happen to be that person, take the opportunity to assure them that we all have these feelings and that it's normal to have anxious thoughts or emotions.

Help Them Get Enough Sleep and Exercise

Your child's overall health plays a great role in how much peace of mind they're getting. If they don't feel peaceful enough, their body and mind won't handle their mental state's ups and downs. It's extremely important to keep reminding them to get enough sleep at night. They should be sleeping from 7 to 8 hours every night. Sleeping for longer or shorter periods could cause headaches and even ruin their mood. They should eat vegetables, whole grains, fruit, and lean protein to provide their bodies with long-term energy rather than the short bursts they get from eating too much sugar or drinking caffeine. If possible, exercise-ing will help them relieve stress and cope with their anxious feelings.

Help Them Spend More Time Out in Nature

Nothing can help you feel more peaceful and grounded than a quiet walk in the park, or maybe a hike in the woods, because nature is simply the quickest medicine for anxiety and feeling overwhelmed. It would be very helpful to encourage your teen to get outside, choose somewhere they find safe and relaxing, and engage more with nature. Your teen can use this opportunity to exercise, try trail biking, or even snowshoeing to release some of their energy and decrease stress and tension.

Consequences of Teen Anxiety

Panic Attacks

Panic attacks happen due to another disorder called Panic Disorder. Many teenagers have another anxiety disorder along with their panic disorder, which causes patients to experience panic attacks, constant feelings of anxiety, and terror. They may also experience physical symptoms, such as chest pain, heart palpitations, and shortness of breath. Panic attacks can strike an anxious patient at any time, so a coping technique is crucial to ending these episodes whenever they occur.

Central Nervous System Damage

If a person suffers from anxiety and panic attacks for a long period, their brains regularly release stress hormones. This reaction causes anxiety and panic symptoms, such as dizziness, headaches, and depression, to become more frequent. When your teen feels stressed or anxious, their brain produces significant amounts of chemicals and hormones designed to prepare the body for threats. Although stress hormones can help them handle stressful situations and events, long-term exposure to these chemicals can be harmful to their bodies and contribute to weight gain.

Excretory and Digestive System Problems

Did you know that anxiety also impacts your child's digestive and excretory system? If your teen has an anxiety disorder, they may experience nausea, stomachaches, diarrhea, and many other digestion-related issues. They may even lose their appetite and start shedding weight rapidly. Some studies show a relation between anxiety and irritable bowel syndrome or IBS, causing your teen to suffer from constipation, diarrhea, and vomiting. In some cases, anxiety can lead to serious gastric issues that cause abdominal discomfort and vomiting.

Immune System Deficiency

When you face a threatening or stressful situation, your anxiety triggers a fight-or-flight process that increases your breathing and pulse rate to get more oxygen to your brain. Your brain does that by flooding hormones and chemicals into your system. Although these chemicals can boost your immune system temporarily, they can weaken it in the long run and cause you to become vulnerable to viral infections and illnesses. If you constantly feel stressed or experience anxiety for a long time, your body never returns to normal functioning, even if the stress passes. This is what anxiety can do to your teenager if you leave it untreated for too long.

Why Are Teens Prone to Anxiety?

As a multitasking parent or adult, you might wonder why teens have to be anxious all the time or what can stress them that much. They don't have to worry about paying rent, putting food on the table, raising children, or any adult responsibilities. So, what causes them to be so vulnerable to anxiety and panic disorders? Maybe, if you knew the reason, you could offer help and ease your son's or daughter's struggles. Therefore, it's important to acknowledge the factors in their life that make this stage difficult and stressful for them. Here are some of these factors.

Brain Development and Hormones

A teenager's brain is not fully developed until they reach their mid-twenties, making it hard for your teen to take on adult responsibilities. Suddenly, they're required to look after themselves when they don't have the brain development or skills necessary to care for themselves fully. Teenagers and younger adults face many moments when they don't know what they are doing. Add to that the tremendous frustration and lack of ability that come along with adulting. It significantly increases your teenager's anxiety levels and causes their hormonal levels to fluctuate, leading them to experience depression, anger, or even anxiety for no reason.

High Expectations and Parental Disapproval

Teenagers go through an endless cycle of stress due to the amount of pressure they put on themselves by building high expectations or trying to match society's expectations of them. They want to do great in school, go to a prestigious university, and participate in all the social events around them. They get parttime jobs, volunteer in community events, finish their chores at home and manage to maintain active social lives. Such expectations can stress your teenager and leave them with no time to sleep or even have a quiet time on their own. They also experience one of the most awkward stages of their lives where they want to meet their parents' expectations and rebel against their authority simultaneously.

Anxiety is very normal at this stage of your teen's life. Keep reminding yourself of this. Teenagers go through one of the toughest periods of their life. They meet new stressful situations and face new challenges impacting their bodies in all sorts of ways. They also have to keep up with your expectations and fit in with their peers to avoid peer pressure. It can drop a heavy burden on your 14 or 15-year-old's shoulders and cause them to develop an anxiety disorder. This is when your role as a parent must accommodate their needs and become their source of comfort. Understand this age carefully and find trusted resources to learn about anxiety disorders that specifically relate to teenagers. It will help you interfere in their routines healthily without causing them any additional stress.

CHAPTER 3

HOW SOCIETY CONTRIBUTES TO YOUR TEEN'S ANXIETY

Society plays a major role in elevating every teen's anxiety and placing unwanted pressure that impacts their short and long-term health. Since puberty is a difficult period to deal with, teens are on the brink of developing anxiety, depression, or other mental health issues.

Questions related to the causes of teenage anxiety, signs, short and long-term effects, and the correlation between shyness and anxiety arise among parents. This chapter will address some important and thought-provoking instances related to society's contribution to teens' anxiety. Since most teens fail to understand or convey their thoughts and feelings, it is time to debunk some myths related to society's impact on teens.

What are the Main Causes of Teen Anxiety?

While several aspects can trigger the effects of stress and anxiety among teens and young adults, it all boils down to the societal impact and its whimsical brunt. Let's take a look at some common causes propelled by the menacing face of our communities.

1. Societal and Peer Pressure

Unwanted peer pressure and the need to be perfect stems from society's grotesque expectations. Extreme emphasis on looking pretty, tall, and perfect can affect a teen's mental health and shake their confidence. They are already undergoing several physical changes, such as a shift in vocal range, height, recurring acne, body odor, sexual urges, etc. It becomes too much to handle, especially since it is new for adolescents. Even though there is no "said" societal pressure, teens get the urge to feel pressured through the fear of judgment and comparison with their friends. This comparison can lead to teens taking drastic steps, too.

Furthermore, the increasing rate of violence, bullying and open threats can also take a toll on the young and developing minds. Traumatic incidents like school shootings, attacks, protests, etc., are alarming and can easily intimidate children and teens. The world we live in is a scary place, and the menace, directly and indirectly, influences young minds. At the same time, society and parents fail to provide coping strategies to help teens face and overcome such challenging situations. Growing up in such a volatile environment will undeniably add to any child's or teen's anxiety.

2. Disapproval from Parents and the Elderly

Teens and young adults are always on their parents' radar as they expect them to succeed and get good grades. The need to get into a good university, establish a successful career, look presentable, etc., are common forms of expectations that most parents have of their teens. However, every person is different, and while some may achieve good grades even without studying, others may fail despite working hard. Parents must examine this threshold and ponder over the legitimate issue instead of putting more stress on the young minds. Like adults, teens have become extremely busy and are expected to participate in sports, volunteer, complete house chores, and study at the same time.

Most parents feel competitive and push their children to perform better. At times, these expectations cross the line and thrust their kids into a mental dilemma. While excelling at school and university is a milestone most teens and parents set, the inability to do so may push the adolescents into a downward spiral. If they keep failing and cannot cope with the stress, they may receive disappointing grunts and disapproval from their parents. Even if the teen wishes to follow a consistent pace, the outlook they receive can steadily turn into anxiety, and this leads to sleep deprivation, which can worsen the situation.

3. Hormonal Changes

Since teens undergo many hormonal changes during the adolescent phase, they may also experience changes in their mental health. Issues, such as depression, stress, anxiety, etc., advance and ebb throughout this delicate phase and invade any teen's lifestyle. Teens are often seen as irritated and angry, especially with their parents. Hormonal fluctuations, testosterone and estrogen surges, menstrual shifts, etc., are some phenomena that are already too difficult to deal with. Since this development phase is new for teens, they cannot decipher the right way to handle it, and it results in passive-aggressiveness and arguments with their loved ones.

Moreover, most teens are immature and unable to confront their feelings, and when paired with mental health fluctuations, the situation can worsen and create anxiety. The responses and reactions are majorly heightened and are upheaved with external stimulants like unsupportive parents and societal peer pressure. All these factors combined can elevate stress hormone receptors, affecting their mental health. Simultaneously, hormones responsible for relaxation and happiness start depleting, adding to the existing discord. It is believed that hormonal changes are one of the major reasons for teenage anxiety and increasing stress.

4. Vices

The stigma that most teens are exposed to during this phase is the use of alcohol, cigarettes, and drugs. Even though they know that their parents will not support this behavior and disapprove of such acts, they still take up drinking and drug usage. While some do drugs and drink alcohol under their friends' influence, others simply wish to experiment. In the latter scenario, it can turn into a long-lasting habit that becomes difficult to overcome.

Teens are easily influenced by the people who are part of their lives. If they hang out with friends who are a bad influence, they are highly likely to pick up similar vices and bad habits. Let's talk about their definition of being "cool." Being cool is shrouded by teen angst. They wish to look and feel grown up physically and mentally. Teens believe that this will earn them respect and help them gain the attention of the opposite gender. They define their curiosity and eagerness to mature fast as being cool. Since adults often drink and smoke, teens get caught up in the same spiral. The situation can be even more threatening if the teens see their parents regularly drinking and smoking. In extreme cases, this can turn into a major addiction and ruin an individual's life. When deprived of cigarettes or alcohol, an addicted person will experience severe anxiety.

5. Immaturity and Brain Development

It is known that a person's brain fully develops once they cross their twenties, and the reason most teens are immature and unable to take care of themselves and others around them. They talk back, are disrespectful, cannot distinguish right from wrong, and are usually frustrated. Since managing and completing certain tasks on their own is difficult, their agitation can steadily turn into anxiety. At times, this can also keep them apart from their loved ones.

Parents often complain about feeling distant from their teens since they prefer to hang out with their friends and stay out until late at night. The feeling of being secluded and grown apart can be too difficult for parents to accept, especially if their child has been extremely close to them in the past. At times, it can reflect in the parents' behavior, which increases their child's anxiety. Teens need their space, and when deprived of it, they will feel anxious.

Paired with the physical and body changes that most teens go through, it can take a major toll on their mental health. Their immaturity also leads them to talk back and disrespect adults. Teens with strict parents may often get punished for their crude behavior, which worsens the situation.

6. Depression

Teenage depression is quite common and is steadily turning into a scenario that affects their adult years as well. The link between societal pressure and depression or anxiety is profoundly intertwined. While some believe that the long-lasting effects of anxiety can lead to depression, others claim that the opposite is also true. Due to this, the symptoms of both issues often overlap, making the diagnosis process even more challenging. Parents often cannot decipher the real issue and fail to understand what their child is going through during their adolescent phase. In any case, anxiety and depression in teens are deep-rooted and should be taken extremely seriously.

Some common symptoms related to depression are constant frustration, irritability, fatigue, feeling hopeless or sad, being alone or isolated, sleeping too much or too little, low concentration levels, headaches, and even suicidal thoughts.

The Impact of Social Media on Teenage Anxiety

Another major reason for teens to feel anxious is the virtual pressure created by social media. The virtual appreciation and validation they receive on social media turn into short-term gratification where most teens find pleasure in.

In extreme cases, social media can ruin a teen's selfesteem as everything seems perfect in the virtual world. They fail to differentiate between reality and virtual representation. In other words, their general sense of worldview can drastically change, leading to constant comparison and unhappiness.

Like the teens of today coin the abbreviation "FOMO," the Fear of Missing Out on the latest updates or trends and not being online is detrimental to their mental health, and this is also why we see teens spending more time on social media instead of studying.

Impact of Anxiety on Teens

Poor Sleeping Habits

This is a common sign among most teens who suffer from anxiety. Recurring thoughts and constant fidgeting keep them awake at night and filling their brains with unwanted thoughts. This behavior also stems from overthinking and digging into the past. They may keep recalling embarrassing moments or argue with themselves about how they could have debated winning an argument more effectively. Even though these are common signs with both teens and adults, obsessive thinking is dangerous and affects their sleeping patterns. In extreme cases, teens with anxiety will develop insomnia affecting their short and longterm health and increases stress.

Poor Eating Habits

Not all teens care about their food habits. They may binge on sugar and hog on chips when they feel bored or unhappy, redirecting their anxious thoughts towards eating, which affects their health in the long run. For instance, while some may have anorexia and lose a lot of weight within a short period, others gain weight due to binge eating. The sudden fluctuations in body weight are extremely unhealthy and worsen their anxiety due to an improper body image. Let's not forget that most teens are anxious about their body weight and beauty issues. Teens with chronic anxiety may also consistently complain about stomach aches, headaches, and other health issues, that emerge from poor eating and sleeping habits.

Low Grades and Performance in School

Some may even feel overwhelmed by the pressure of completing their tasks on time leading to poor grades and low performance in school and university. The inability to perform better in school also stems from extra peer pressure and unreasonably high expectations from parents. Even if the child is trying hard, they may not get the anticipated scores, which aggravates their anxiety. They will also be compared to the teens who perform well and get the best grades adding to their anxiety. Along with getting poor scores, they may also show indiscipline, such as skipping school or tardiness.

Getting into Trouble

Teens often get in trouble and unnecessary fights over petty issues. However, if it turns into a consistent pattern, it can result from some deeper dispute. In essence, this disruptive behavior is a coping mechanism that is displayed to a varying degree. While some may cope with their anxiety by showcasing poor sleeping or eating habits, others display disruptive behavior and get in trouble from time to time. You will constantly receive complaints related to unnecessary tiffs and even punching or throwing things from your teen's school. At home, they are likely to throw tantrums and talk back. In such cases, it is difficult for the parent to control their child, which is why learning about the signs of anxiety and treating it from the initial stages is more helpful.

Boredom or Feeling Unexcited

Being bored and not feeling excited about anything is another byproduct of anxiety. The feeling of not doing anything and lying in bed with recurring thoughts is something most teens are guilty of. Irritability, frustration, and agitation are common side effects of feeling bored. Since they prefer to be alone and hardly step out the boredom increases. In essence, boredom and anxiety are cohesive, and one can lead to the other. It is believed that agitated restlessness, anxiety, and boredom are interconnected. Even though the tedium-inducing effects are not well-defined by researchers to date, they can definitely make an impact on every teen's imagination power, creativity, concentration levels, and productivity.

The correlation of boredom with anxiety can be distinctively laid out in two different viewpoints. In the first case, boredom can make a person extremely lazy and lethargic, to the point that they cannot keep their eyes open, resulting in prolonged hours of sleep. On the contrary, being bored can result in restlessness and constant fidgeting. The second case is highly relevant to chronic anxiety and is expressed through signs like tapping your feet, pacing in the hallway, or feeling confused. Even though you try to concentrate and attempt to finish a task, the surging thoughts may stop you. With the drawback and lack of concentration, some people may even develop relevant mental issues, such as attention-deficit hyperactivity disorder (ADHD).

Social Isolation

As mentioned earlier, social isolation may also emerge from anxiety and result in social anxiety disorder. Teens who fear not being likable or constantly judged are more prone to developing this form of anxiety disorder. Simple things like receiving glances when eating or shaking hands when meeting new people can make them super anxious. It will shake their confidence and deteriorate their communication skills. The feeling of being rejected when making small mistakes can eat them up from inside. It is more dreadful than we think it is. Dodging fear is a natural phenomenon that most humans proactively seek. However, considering actual people as a threat when they mean no harm to you makes the matter serious. Unable to cope with this challenge, most teens get into a "fight or flight" mode that can result in social isolation and loneliness.

Long-term Effects of Anxiety on Teens

Substance Use and Addiction

While trying to drink and smoke once or twice is a common phenomenon among most teens, prolonged use leads to addiction, which can ruin their lives.

Depression

As mentioned, when left untreated for a prolonged period, anxiety can steadily turn into depression and push the teen into misery. At times, depression can linger for many years and also ruin their adult life.

Suicidal Thoughts

With anxiety and depression, some teens may compile all the thoughts together, leading to suicidal intentions. The fear of being judged, the inability to perform better at school, failing to meet their parents' expectations, societal pressure, etc., can pile up and impose an overwhelming feeling. Those without parental support or lack of motivation may find it easier to leave the world than deal with their day-to-day qualms. It may seem ridiculous, but some teens are also anxious about the thought of the world ending. With the rising pandemic crisis, violence, climate change, and other major issues surrounding young children and teens' delicate minds, some take it acutely.

Causes of Shyness or Nervousness in Teens

Even though being shy or nervous isn't necessarily a bad sign, it can affect a teen's personality and hinder their communication skills at a social level. The main cause of shyness, timidness, or nervousness is low self-confidence or self-esteem. Shyness is yet another form of coping mechanism that shouldn't be encouraged in teens. While genetics and the environment they grow up in are the main factors resulting in teens being shy, the people they hang out with and peer pressure also play a major role. More importantly, low self-esteem can result in passive behavior that keeps teens from speaking up, even if they know they are not being treated right. In the long run, it can also affect their personal and professional life. Teens with passive behavior believe that their opinions don't matter and lack decision-making skills, and this can result from a poor upbringing or inspired by the negative qualities of their parents.

Are You Born with Social Anxiety? Does It Ever Go Away?

No one is born with social anxiety. In essence, inheriting relevant genetic traits can make the problem more intense. Stress, nervousness, and social phobia arise due to other factors as a person grows up but is elevated with the inherited genetics making it difficult to treat. When treated correctly, social anxiety does pass with time. Some people confuse social anxiety with awkwardness. While the former is steadily built due to several factors, the latter is a personality trait that can be difficult to overcome. By building confidence in teens and motivating them, they can surpass this social anxiety phase and elevate their communication skills.

Key Takeaway: The hideous truth of society's negative impact on teen anxiety is amiably cloaked by words like apprehension and expectations. As you can see, one anxiety-related issue is connected to other mental health problems. Failing to curb anxiety and the signs that follow can majorly disrupt your teen's mental health and quality of life. Since every teen portrays different signs of anxiety and copes with it using varying strategies, deciphering and handling the issue can be more challenging for the parent. While some teens may throw tantrums, others may completely isolate themselves. Social media adds to the existing issue and makes the situation formidable.

CHAPTER 4

HOW PARENTS CONTRIBUTE TO TEEN ANXIETY

It is a long-established fact that the environment in which we live directly affects our mental health. Since parents take up a huge part of their teen's life, naturally, they can significantly affect their teen's anxiety. Even if your child spends most of their time in their bedroom or outside of the house, you are automatically associated with their idea of what a home should be. A home is supposed to be a comfort zone and a safe haven, but unfortunately, for teens that struggle with anxiety, a home can often be perceived as a trigger. The extent to which you are involved or uninvolved in your teen's life can feed into their anxiety. Words, actions, and behavior that may seem innocent and habitual can stimulate their anxiety, too. Living with an anxious teen is not easy and can sometimes be frustrating. However, once you truly understand how their minds work, acknowledge their fears, and explore your actions, you will realize that their train of thought is a justifiable response.

Living with anxiety can be a nightmare for the most part. With the growing number of teens diagnosed with anxiety disorders, it can be very easy for some parents to believe that their child's mental illness is their fault. When approaching your teen's anxiety, it's important to remember that you are not to blame for their disorder. Though, you should also keep in mind that some of your parenting habits may add to the problem. As a parent of an anxious teen, accept that you can either continue being part of the problem or step up to become part of the solution. Taking accountability and admitting that some of your actions may not be in your child's best interest is not easy. However, it is the first step toward relieving some of the pressure off your teen. This chapter will explore how you may be unintentionally hurting your teen and how you can help them.

How Parents Can Give Teens Anxiety

Too Caring

When it comes to your child's anxiety and emotions, it is important to remember that not everyone is the same. If one thing triggers a teen's anxiety, it does not necessarily mean that it negatively affects your child. Your best bet is to explore the different possibilities and closely recall how your child reacts in certain situations. Surprisingly, some teens get anxious when their parents care too much. Showing empathy when your child experiences a hurtful or heartbreaking situation is only normal. However, for some children, too much empathy is distressing. If you have noticed that your teen has suddenly stopped sharing things with you, especially their troubles, it's probably because of how you reacted to these situations in the past. It doesn't mean that you must stop showing that you care. It just means that you should show fewer signs of worry and anguish. If your teen decides to share their worries with you only to find that you're also worried, it will make things worse for them. The best thing to do is remain strong for them instead of falsely communicating to them that anxiety is the only way to face the issue. Besides, keeping their worries to themselves will further set off their anxiety.

Extreme Advocating

Another way you may be accidentally giving your teen anxiety is by taking it to the extreme when advocating for them. Every child finds comfort in the fact that their parents stand up for them no matter what. Similarly, standing up for your child is a parental instinct. However, don't forget that teens value their space, freedom, and independence now more than ever. Your eagerness to stand up for them when they didn't ask you to or explicitly asked you not to can raise their anxiety levels. Your persistence to advocate for them can break their self-confidence and show them that you don't believe they can resolve their issues on their own, leading them to avoid confiding in you. Your first instinct shouldn't be rushing to advocate on their behalf but rather to help them find a solution. Let them know that you believe they'll eventually resolve it on their own.

Focusing On Weaknesses

Every parent wants to help their child tackle their weaknesses. While this type of support may be needed at times, it can easily become overbearing. Your teen doesn't want you to sign them up for private tutoring after getting one bad grade or buying them a motivational book when they feel down. Although this may be done with good intentions, your teen will automatically focus on the negative aspects. To boost their confidence and ease their anxiety, encourage them to play on their strengths instead of focusing on their weaknesses. One bad grade doesn't mean that they're weak at a certain subject. Even if they were, let them know that they don't have to be great at everything. Teach them to be content enough with what they are good at, reminding them that everyone has their own strengths and weaknesses. If your child likes to paint, offer to enroll them in professional painting classes.

Enhancing their skills is better than trying to work on their weaknesses. It will give them a great confidence boost, which may even carry over to their weak points.

Overemphasizing Strengths

We mentioned above that you should focus on your teens' strengths and encourage them to enhance them. However, be aware that there's a very thin line between encouragement and expectations. When you over-encourage or overly show off your child, they may feel like you are setting very high expectations for them, and this will provoke their anxiety and may even lead them to lose interest in this specific skill. Telling your friends that your teen is going to become a world-famous artist or gymnast is pressuring. Compliment them when they excel, though, don't make them feel like you are expecting more.

Fear of Disappointment

All parents work very hard to ensure their children have great values and morals. Encouraging good values is extremely important and is something that any parent must do. Be that as it may, you must know where to draw the line. Stressing over certain values can result in your child obsessing over them. They may associate these values with their identity. On top of that, if they mess up, they will feel they have let you and themself down. Teens are susceptible to making poor choices. However, they should never feel too anxious to talk to you about them.

Can Controlling Parents Cause Anxiety?

A teenager's autonomy and sense of control may be their ultimate desire. To most teens, control and freedom may be among the things they value the most in life. The majority of anxious teens feel the need to control their surroundings to feel at peace. Feeling out of control can cause anxiety to eat away at them, and controlling parents may be one of the causes. There are many ways to express love, and to some parents, being overly controlling is one way. Controlling parents don't necessarily exert control over their children to make their lives miserable. They do it because they think they know what's best for them. However, this excessive control can severely damage their child's mental, emotional, and social health.

Control comes in many forms. It can be behavioral or psychological and internal or external. Behavioral control is when a parent is determined to monitor their teen's social life, whereabouts, and behavior. When you exert this type of control over your teen, you are unnecessarily creating trust issues. Your child will constantly feel that you don't trust them and will always feel afraid that they may be doing something wrong- even when they're not. This type of control leaves them living in a constant state of anxiety. Psychological control is when a parent invades their teen's emotional and psychological state or development. Many parents with teens with mental disorders often validate their child's psychological issues. For instance, the majority of depressed teens are surrounded by family members who believe they are melodramatic or ungrateful. Similarly, children with anxiety have to suffer in silence because their parents tell them that their worries are silly. This type of control manipulates a child's psychological experience and causes them to believe that their feelings and mental health are not valid, further worsening their anxiety. You don't have to express verbal or external control to trigger your child. Internal control, such as expressing feelings of shame or guilt, is enough to hurt them.

There are many things that parents do daily without realizing that it's an eminent form of control. If you expect your child to obey you blindly and don't allow your teen to question or participate in decisions that affect them, then you are a controlling parent. Not allowing them to make their own decisions, discouraging them from becoming independent, and helping them without their permission can also severely break their confidence. If you prevent them from participating in certain activities because you "said so," it may cause them to act out. Using manipulations, such as love withdrawals and guilt-tripping, using punishments as a form of discipline, and constantly criticizing them will likely cause them to exhibit anti-social behavior and high anxiety tendencies.

How Can Parents' Stress Hurt a Child?

Many comprehensive research and studies suggest that a parent's behavior can greatly affect a child's mental health. Mental illnesses are not developed overnight, but they are an accumulation of several thoughts, feelings, and observations over the years. Like most things, behavior and responses are taught. For example, if anger is your response to a specific situation, your child will be conditioned that this is how they should act when they find themselves in a similar circumstance. A stressed parent can affect an anxious child in a stage that's as early as pregnancy. A stressed pregnant woman can give birth to a child with several behavioral and psychological problems, including anxiety, ADHD, mood disorders, and risk for autism spectrum disorder. Stressed parents during the first few years of a child's life affect the child's genes. The signs resulting from such alterations, such as negative impacts on brain development and insulin production, can show throughout their later years and adolescence.

When you are stressed, you're likely to trigger a fight or flight response, which is the same response that is activated when someone is feeling anxious. Tension and anxiety are very closely related, so your teen will also certainly be on edge when you are constantly stressed. Parents who fight a lot, creating a stressful and tense atmosphere, are more likely to have children who show signs of depression and anxiety. A role of a parent in their teen's life is, directly and indirectly, incredibly significant.

The best thing you can do for your child, no matter how old they are or the developmental stage they're in, is to provide them with a sense of calmness, safety, and the lack of stress. Some studies show that perhaps this is even more important than providing them with unconditional love and emotions. This sense of tranquility allows their brains to develop and function in a familiar environment, resulting in a normally wired brain. Brains that develop in a constant state of stress are wired to always be prepared for an ambiguous sense of crippling danger, causing your child to be constantly anxious.

What Are Signs of Bad Parenting?

In most cases, parents, and their parenting habits, are a great contributory factor to teens' anxiety. Adopting bad parenting habits doesn't automatically make you a bad parent. Bad parents are parents who realize that their actions are negatively impacting their child yet choose to do nothing about it. Being a parent is a 24/7 job that doesn't come with a handbook or clear guidelines, so it's normal to feel like parenting efforts are below par. The problem with being a parent is that every choice matters, and every mistake can result in long-term effects. If you feel like you may be doing something wrong, the following are bad parenting signs to watch out for.

Being Over or Under Involved

Determining how involved you should be in your teen's life is very tricky. You don't want to be in the dark, not knowing anything about your child, and risk having them get themselves in severe trouble. On the other hand, you don't want to be involved to the extent where they feel suffocated. As long as you don't neglect your child's basic needs or take complete control of their decisions, trust that you will find the right balance. Establish trust and boundaries, and navigate until you find something that works for you and your child. Aim to become your child's friend and get involved because they want you to be one of the best things to happen to them.

Little or Rigid Discipline

Like involvement in your child's life, you need to find the right balance for discipline. Undisciplined children don't understand boundaries, which creates many problems for them as they grow up. Undisciplined adolescents can often get themselves into great trouble. Children who lack discipline typically look after themselves at a very young age. Meanwhile, parents who overly discipline their children or enforce rigid and strict discipline prevent their children from creating their own journeys and experiences, resulting in either an extremely rebellious child or a very anxious one. Therefore, teach your child about what's wrong and right, and explain the consequences and the rewards. The best you can do is be there for your child and be someone who they can talk to about their fears, failures, adventures, and mistakes.

Attention and Affection Withdrawal

One fatal mistake that many parents make is associating their child's mistakes with expressing their feelings towards them. Ignoring your child and withdrawing feelings of affection from them when they do something wrong only shows them that your love for them is conditional. Your child will live their life in anxiety, believing that you will stop loving them if you don't approve of their actions or life choices. Doing this to your child will also lower their confidence and self-esteem. They may also develop codependency tendencies, leading to involvement in abusive relationships.

How a Parent Can Help a Teen with Anxiety

As hard as it may be, one of your duties as a parent is to help your child navigate through all sorts of hardships. If you have a child with anxiety, you probably realize the magnitude of the issue. Knowing that your teen is struggling with all of these thoughts and emotions can be greatly disheartening. However, you must know that anxiety is very common, especially during the teen years. As a parent, you must teach your teen that anxiety management is a very important life skill. Everyone gets anxious at some point, though the intensity of the emotions differs. Luckily, there are multiple ways you can help your child manage their anxiety.

Facing Anxiety

One of the best ways to deal with anxiety is learning how to face it. When you are anxious, you have no other option than to live through these tormenting emotions. Since anxiety disorders are frightening, learning how to tackle the situation is a great help. When attempting to help a teen with anxiety, you must listen and acknowledge their fears and understand that their thoughts and emotions are valid even when they don't sound that grave or realistic to you. Take your child seriously and offer them the support they need. Encourage them to do the things that they're anxious about without pushing them too hard. Help them set small goals and avoid taking control of the situation. If your teen decides to avoid a certain activity because they're anxious, do not shame them for it. Help them manage their feelings or reassure them that they can manage them in the future.

Exploring Feelings

Most of the time, people who suffer from anxiety don't know what they're anxious about exactly. If your teen gets anxious all of a sudden, help them to break down their emotions. Walking them through recent events to identify the trigger also helps. It will help them understand their feelings and, ultimately, manage their anxiety, allowing them to avoid such situations in the future.

Love and Support

Teens who suffer from anxiety can feel burdensome. They realize that they're not easy to deal with, which is also something that adds to their distress. Show your child constant love and support, as this helps them cope with their anxiety better. Set a good example for your child by managing your stress and anxiety.

Calming an Anxious Child

Before exploring emotions, you must, first, calm your child down. Coming up with distractions or offering to engage in a fun activity can help them feel at ease. You can also practice deep breathing together or use the grounding method. If possible, take them for a walk or a run since fresh air can help them calm down.

Teenagers are at a high risk of developing mental disorders, such as anxiety and depression.

Such illnesses are not easy to deal with and are stigmatized in several societies. People who don't have anxiety often find it hard to understand or acknowledge an anxious person's thoughts and emotions. However, if you are the parent of an anxious child, you must learn how to navigate this hardship with them.

CHAPTER 5

WHAT TO DO IF MY TEEN HAS ANXIETY?

By now, you should clearly understand and decipher the signs related to anxiety, stress, and related mental health issues. This chapter will divide the common signs of anxiety based on selective characteristics to help you seek medical help and treatment options accordingly. By the end of this chapter, you will be able to recognize and treat anxiety-related signs, manage the situation, and take immediate action before it worsens.

Common Signs of Anxiety

Even though we discussed the most prominent signs of anxiety in the previous chapter, we can further understand the symptoms in detail by categorizing them for easier diagnosis. The common signs of anxiety can be interpreted through emotional, physical, and behavioral phenomena.

Emotional Signs of Anxiety

Feeling on Edge

The continuous racing thoughts and feeling irritated are signs that your child is "feeling on edge." They may also not be able to address their feelings and emotions, let alone share them with others. Common signs of feeling on edge include emotional distress and being burned out. The constant guilt of not finishing tasks and the inability to begin working on them make your teen feel even more distressed, leading to this feeling of being on edge. If your teen freaks out when they think or talk about the future and their dreams, they may need help eliminating these feelings. It often leads the person to cause self-harm and hurt themselves.

Constant Mood Swings

Do not mistake constant mood swings with hormonal changes. While hormones may play a major role in affecting your teen's mood, feeling the same way for a longer period can indicate a more serious health issue. Withdrawal symptoms, substance use, and anxiety disorders are often responsible for shifts in a teen's mood. Some mood disorders that teens are exposed to include bipolar disorder, major depressive disorder (MDD), disruptive mood dysregulation disorder (DMDD), cyclothymic disorder, personality disorder, and dysthymia. However, not all are related to anxiety, and they may have similar signs, making it difficult to diagnose the actual issue.

Continuous Restlessness

If your teen sways from one place to another and refuses to settle in one place, they can be deemed restless. It often results from constant worrying and feeling nervous about their situation.

Even though it might not necessarily be bad or harmful, your anxious teen may second-guess themselves and make it harder for them to accept reality. Another reason that can cause restlessness is the constant fear of bad things happening, even if they are less likely to occur. If your teen often thinks about the future and fears failing or not excelling at what they do, they may suffer from restlessness and anxiety.

How to Treat Emotional Signs of Anxiety

An effective way to treat emotional signs that occur due to anxiety is journaling or keeping a diary. Encourage your child to keep a diary and write down their thoughts without feeling hesitant. Not all teens will be willing to document their thoughts on paper, but encouraging them will stimulate their brain. Provide the assurance of letting them keep their diary locked up. The assertion on privacy will motivate them to try this tactic. The idea is to decode a pattern of the teen's emotional journey and mood changes on a day-to-day basis.

As soon as your teen experiences signs of irritability or a major mood swing, ask them to note it down in their diary. Ask them to continue noting down their changes in feelings, mood, and thoughts over 2 weeks to cipher a pattern. With time, your child will be able to deduce signs of negative feelings and be prepared to face them instead of being anxious and panicking. Ask them to jot down positive feelings, too, as it will help them rate their irritability on a scale of 0 to 10.

The things and feelings that caused supreme anxiety can then be recognized as "triggers." This exercise may seem simple, but it is extremely effective as part of early diagnosis.

Physical Warning Signs of Anxiety

1. Stomach and Gastrointestinal Issues

Anxiety and gastrointestinal issues are closely linked. Patients with recurring stomach issues are often checked for anxiety disorders and depression because any issue related to the abdomen and stomach is known to increase stress. It is also believed that the condition of the gut can impact stress levels. Prominent signs, such as trouble digesting food, diarrhea, constipation, abdominal cramps, and nausea, are commonly witnessed when suffering from gastrointestinal and stomach problems. Do not ignore these signs as they can be related to more serious anxiety disorders, such as panic disorder, social anxiety disorder (SAD), or phobia.

2. Sudden Weight Changes

As discussed in the previous chapter, sudden changes in body weight are also signs of anxiety and can be related to mental health issues. If your child has recently undergone excessive weight gain or loss, get them checked to detect the actual cause. Since they experience major hormonal changes during puberty, bodily changes are also common. However, if you see different signs related to weight issues, such as excessive eating, binge eating, changes in eating patterns, etc., in your teens, then monitor their food and eating habits. Since anxiety and eating disorders are closely related, watching what your teen eats and offering help is of the utmost importance.

3. Migraines

People suffering from stress and anxiety are also likely to experience headaches and migraines. While suffering from a headache once in a while shouldn't be a major concern, pay attention to your teen's condition if they frequently complain about recurring headaches. If a teenager has been addicted to alcohol, cigarettes, or drugs, they may also experience withdrawal symptoms when quitting. Relevant signs include a racing heart, restlessness, and headaches. In extreme cases, seeking medical help can alleviate symptoms and reduce stress levels in your teen. You can also consider the option of placing them in rehab if the situation gets out of control. At times, your teen may feel muscle spasms or pains as the body gets extremely tense in stressful situations.

Researchers also claim that prolonged anxiety-related issues can cause serious health issues, such as back and vision problems and even asthma.

How to Treat Physical Signs of Anxiety

The simplest way to alleviate anxiety symptoms that physically affect your teen is by focusing on improving their physical endurance and incorporating changes to enhance body image. Begin with a daily, slow-paced, 30-minute walk early in the morning. Walking outside is highly recommended as it allows your teens time to reflect on their thoughts and put them together. It is also an effective relaxation technique that can help calm your child's mind. With time, encourage them to join aerobics or Pilates classes as this will also treat and train your child's muscles and relieve tension in delicate parts. In a nutshell, being active and focusing on physical movements will divert their attention and reduce stress.

When it comes to treating rapid breathing or the inability to breathe, teach some effective breathing techniques to your teen to cope with the situation instantly. It will prevent them from developing major breathing issues like asthma and calm their senses within a jiffy. Regulating proper sleep is also important as stress and improper sleeping patterns are closely related. Ensure that your teen has at least 7 to 8 hours of sound sleep. It will significantly improve their physical and mental health.

Behavioral Manifestations of Anxiety

1. Procrastination

Another recurring effect of anxiety is procrastination, feeling lost, and the inability to concentrate. Staying restless and experiencing recurring negative thoughts leads to distraction, which eventually leads to procrastination. As you know, a teen with an anxiety disorder is highly likely to be lethargic and will keep delaying their tasks due to the fear of failing. Even though the task may take just a few hours to complete, your anxious teen may keep delaying it for weeks or even months.

2. Poor Performance

Lacking focus and procrastinating eventually leads to poor performance in school and resulting in low grades. Regularly skipping school also affects your teen's performance. Ensure they attend classes and feel at ease when they're studying or preparing for their tests. Skipping school and getting low grades are also related to the physical changes and anxiety of your teen. If they are sick and unable to complete tasks on time, do their homework, and study, they may have a major downfall of scores, diminishing their chance of getting into a reputed university. Since your teen's high school years are crucial for university entry, they must be pushed back on track.

3. Fear of Staying in Public or Alone

Teens with anxiety either need someone by their side in public places or stay completely isolated. While the former situation may stem from issues like separation anxiety, the latter is a result of social phobia. They will avoid meeting people and stay isolated in their rooms. Even if they go out, they need someone to accompany them in heavily crowded places. Their fear of meeting and talking to people may be misunderstood as rude or awkward behavior. In extreme cases, frequent outbursts are also commonly witnessed by parents. Teens embarrassed with this behavior may turn to compulsive behaviors, such as cleaning, frequent organization, arranging their books until they are satisfied, washing their hands every few hours, etc.

When left untreated, these physical, emotional, and behavioral signs can steadily become a serious issue that is difficult to cure in the long run.

How to Treat Behavioral Signs of Anxiety

Taking some time out to reflect on important thoughts helps alleviate behavioral manifestations related to anxiety. Simple activities, such as listening to music, reading a book, or sipping tea, can calm the mind and provide enough energy to face reality. Encourage your teen to speak up and openly communicate their thoughts and emotions without feeling hesitant. Talk to your child's teacher and prepare a plan based on the signs they display. Since teachers observe and react to different behavioral signs daily, they can help you formulate an effective plan and appropriate treatment for your teen's anxiety.

Based on these categories that define distinct characteristics of anxiety, you can seek help accordingly. While some teens may experience anxiety emotionally, others will display varied behavioral signs.

Common Treatment Options for Anxiety

Once you recognize the signs and comprehend that your teen is suffering from anxiety, take them for a clinical diagnosis, too. Apart from the common coping mechanisms and early diagnosis of anxiety at home, several treatment options are available that can be extremely helpful to treat your child's anxiety and prevalent symptoms.

Breathing and Relaxation Techniques

Breathing techniques are extremely helpful to recover from an anxiety attack instantly. Since the frequency of anxiety attacks varies from person to person, performing breathing exercises reduces the symptom's chances of getting too serious. An anxious person's body is prone to being in a hyperventilation mode, and it can lack consistent flow and oxygen supply, which will worsen the situation as carbon dioxide is known to assist the body's anxious mode. Some may even show signs of shallow over-breathing.

Learning the correct breathing techniques, a teen can switch to breathing from their diaphragm instead of their chest, which helps them calm down within a few minutes. When you breathe in, let your belly expand.

One hand should be placed on the chest and the other on the lower abdomen.

This breathing technique, known as the abdominal breathing technique, is commonly used to treat anxiety and calm the senses. However, several techniques can be considered based on the teen's condition and severity of anxiety. The idea is to take in more oxygen and control its movements throughout the body while expelling carbon dioxide to alleviate stress. The involuntary functions monitored by the body's nervous system understand the deliberate attempt at controlling its breathing pattern and reduces stress. Along with feeling calmer, the body also experiences lower lactic acid levels, improved energy, and proper heart rate.

Mindfulness practices keep your anxious teen's recurring thoughts in control and help them concentrate. Since most teens are troubled due to anxious thoughts affecting their studies, mindfulness significantly alleviates the symptoms. Several exercises related to mindfulness and improved concentration levels can be useful for your teen. Guided imagery, meditation, and visualization techniques are some forms of mindfulness practices that relieve signs of anxiety. You can also try certain isometric relaxation techniques for your teen with the help of an expert.

Cognitive-Behavioral Therapy

This form of therapy is directed towards anxious individuals who cannot gather and face their thoughts, often leading to restlessness and feeling lost. Cognitive therapy uses tools and measures to change a teen's way of thinking and remolding their thought process to cope with stress. In essence, the negative feelings associated with anxiety, also known as triggers, can be effectively overcome with cognitivebehavioral therapy. Most of the time, such triggers make the anxiety worse and can push your teen into a downward spiral. For example, if your teen is suffering from social anxiety and no one pays attention to what they say, they will immediately think they are boring or worthless. This negative thought of feeling worthless is the trigger that can be treated or, at least, mellowed with the help of cognitive therapy.

Some of the impactful strategies and tools that make cognitive therapy useful are cognitive restructuring, attention training, rational, cognitive challenging, and encouraging self-talk. Exposure therapy is the primary strategy used in behavior therapy, helping the teen face their fears and acknowledge them. Since the inability to face fears and ignore them is one reason that triggers negative feelings, eradicating them is the easiest way to overcome this issue. The teen is asked to rank their fears in order of the worst to the least frightening thought and acknowledge each and every part of it.

Even though no actual medical test can firmly and dedicatedly diagnose anxiety, some effective screening tools help you understand your teen's condition and measure the level of anxiety they are facing. Experienced psychologists, counselors, and psychiatrists are well-versed with such screening techniques, which is why you must take your teen for an early screening test and start treatment as soon as possible.

Counseling and Self-Help Group

Talking to a loved one and sharing your thoughts can also help. However, getting your teenage son or daughter to share their thoughts can be a difficult task. In such cases, seek help from counseling and self-help groups directed towards teens who feel worthless and fear meeting new people. It is an effective way to treat social phobia and improve communication skills. In essence, counseling sessions and self-help groups help your child get back on track by building their confidence and self-esteem.

Other signs such as constantly feeling depressed, experiencing mood swings, feeling shameful, etc., can be treated by participating in self-help groups. Some take help from strategies such as structured problem solving, which helps resolve procrastination and puts worrying thoughts at bay. Instead of focusing on what can go bad, your anxious teen will learn to direct their energy towards completing delayed tasks.

Medication

Anxiety is also treated with medication, specifically in extreme situations like recurring anxiety attacks and when the teen has undergone episodes of self-harm. Medication is also considered when therapy hasn't or isn't working for the patient. Even though therapy works most of the time, people diagnosed with a higher level of anxiety may need to take medication along with consistent visits to their psychologist. A set of antidepressants and tranquilizers is often prescribed to patients who suffer from physical issues due to anxiety. Medical practitioners still advise them to undergo therapy to overcome anxiety in the long run.

Physical and Dietary Changes

You can also establish certain physical and dietary lifestyle changes to reduce anxiety-related symptoms. Apart from physical benefits, exercising can boost mental health and treat psychological issues. By introducing effective changes in your teen's diet, you can control their hormone levels and balance cortisol and adrenaline levels. These hormones are responsible for changes in breathing patterns and heartbeat range, and feeding the right type of food can steadily treat the problem.

It is believed that a deficiency of magnesium, calcium and Vitamin B can heighten anxiety and depressionrelated signs. Monitoring the diet based on these supplements then becomes crucial. Certain food items, such as caffeine, salt, and nicotine, should be avoided as they trigger negative emotions. To achieve faster and safe results, consult a certified nutritionist and fitness trainer to customize a diet and exercise plan based on your teen's condition.

Key Takeaway: Anxiety can affect your teen's physical, mental, and emotional health majorly. As you know by now, if you fail to treat anxiety-related symptoms at the earliest, they will worsen and turn into depression or even bipolar disorder. Early diagnosis is possible by looking deep into the signs that your teen displays. Use certain tricks at home to help your teen cope with their issues. If the signs are too serious and untreatable at home, seek help from a therapist and encourage your teen to undergo treatment before it's too late. More importantly, make them feel safe and provide the assurance of staying by their side at all times.

The upcoming chapters will look into treatment options and coping mechanisms in detail to help you get a clearer idea and deal with the issue more adequately.

CHAPTER 6

LEARN ABOUT AND TEACH ANXIETY

It is time to face reality and talk to your teen about what and how they are feeling. This chapter talks about your approach and communication skills when confronting your teen to make them feel at ease and reduce stress. While you do certain things for your anxious teen, you should refrain from uttering specific words and statements as they depreciate their vantage point. It's about being calm, supportive, and affirmative about your child's condition and keeping them assured. As you know by now, there is no right or straightforward approach to treat anxiety. All you can do is respond smartly to help your child cope with the stress and anxiety symptoms lucratively.

Talking to Your Teen about Anxiety

Talking about Fears and Worries

A supportive and patient parent can help treat a teen's anxiety at a faster and steady pace. If your teen is going through a hard time, show them your support and be open to discussion sessions. Be empathetic and compassionate towards your teen, especially when they approach you during a commotion. Do not scold them when they make a mistake. Instead, learn more about the triggers that could have led them to make a mistake.

Here are some questions you can ask your anxious teen to show your support.

- What thoughts do you often get?
- Are you worrying about something? Do you think I can help you with it?
- How are you feeling physically and mentally?

- Are you getting proper sleep?
- Are you eating properly? What foods and drinks do you often crave?
- What is bothering you?
- Is bullying common in your school? Has someone bullied you?
- Are you facing any fears? Are you scared of something?
- Are your friends supportive?

Regularly asking these questions helps you understand your child better and encourages you to design a pattern of their thought process. It not only makes diagnosis easier but also keeps your teen slightly at ease.

Utter words and statements like,

- I understand that the way you feel is terrible.
- I am here for you.
- Do not let your thoughts define you.
- We can get through this.
- You can talk to me about it openly.
- I promise to listen without judgment.
- The situation sounds intense, but you managed it well.

- You are doing your best.
- I care about you deeply.

These pep talk statements are converted into empathetic expressions that are more relatable to your teen. For example, instead of saying, "Be courageous" or "Buck up," be more empathetic and say, "I am extremely sorry you've been going through this" or "being in this state must feel terrible." Such paradoxes provide the reassurance of someone being truly understanding and supportive. Your teen will feel at ease and gather the courage to overcome the situation.

However, converting or reframing your words is not always an effective way to calm your teen. It may not work at all. In such cases, turn to a more realistic non-threatening way to help your child keep up. For example, go for a walk together or spend some time doing things that your child likes. You can also suggest meditation or take Pilates classes together.

Delving Into the World of Anxiety

Initially, you may find your child being too sensitive or stubborn. However, once you delve into the world of anxiety and learn its true connotation, you will unravel the actual dilemma they are facing. When facing unwanted situations, they are just responding through the "fight-flight-freeze" trigger. Just like animals react to unwanted or dangerous circumstances by screeching or attacking the hunter, teens also often throw tantrums or outbursts as a coping mechanism.

In some cases, teens cannot cipher the actual degree of risk and why they get confused or feel lost. They may be unable to tell how dangerous a particular situation is or whether or not it is harmful. They may also rely on their parents to help them understand what they are going through. When they fail to get the support or help they are unconsciously expecting, their anxiety levels increase. As we have been emphasizing throughout this book, your duty as a parent is to recognize the signs, help your child overcome them, and be patient and supportive throughout this ordeal.

Identifying Anxiety

The generation gap between you and your child is wide, and the mindsets are entirely different. You have to understand your child's mindset and dig deeper to perceive their world and situation through their perspective. Acknowledge that your child hates being clingy, stubborn, restless, or falling off the stairs. It is their nervousness and fidgety nature that their anxiety disorder has fathered.

Here is what you need to know about anxiety to help your teen.

- Anxiety is not threatening. Many parents freak out when learning that their teenage child is going through anxiety. If your teen has recently been diagnosed with anxiety, you must know that it can be treated with patience and time. Everyone, at some point in their life, is prone to experiencing anxiety. It's important to understand that early diagnosis and treatment can alleviate relevant symptoms before it turns into a serious problem. However, it is not as dangerous as others claim. Still, it does not mean you can take the matter lightly.

- Anxiety is your body's way of preparing you. As discussed earlier, anxiety is common among people who sense danger around them. In other words, it is your body's way of preparing you to face the fear or danger around you. In some cases, random bursts of anxiety may help your teen perform at their best. However, it shouldn't be experienced for a prolonged period.

- Anxiety can become a problem when it interferes with your teen's day-to-day life. If your teen's anxiety is not allowing them to enjoy the simple pleasures of life or even finish their tasks with ease, it should not be taken lightly. With time, it can turn into distress. Situations like seeing a big dog approaching them or being separated from you for long can easily freak them out. They may also be seen screaming, obsessively biting their nails, picking their hair, or feeling unwell before or during important occasions.

What Not to Do

While being with your anxious teen and supporting them at all times is of the utmost importance, there are certain things that you shouldn't say to them as it can make things worse. Dealing with anxiety is already nerve-wracking for your anxious teen, so saying certain things can create a negative image and phantasm that is difficult to exit. Even though the truth may be harsh to face at this point, it is always better than lying to your teen. Amusingly, the parents who have been through anxiety or are quite rational are the ones who may spit out the wrong words. Since they are more open-minded and practical, they are expected to say the right things and support their child correctly, which is not often the case. The chances of unconsciously dismissing their child's opinions are rather high than targeting the right pool of thoughts.

Here are some things that you should never say to your anxious teen.

It's Not a Big Deal

Stop saying, "Don't sweat it" or "It's not a big deal" to your anxious teen because it actually is something huge and intense that they're going through. Even if it feels like a small issue from your perspective, it may not be as dainty as you think. Instead of illustrating it as a positive or uplifting message, your teen may feel worse since the problem doesn't seem as huge to someone else. It is known that people suffering from anxiety and related symptoms feel things more intensely. For them, every emotion and thought is too big and vehement. Instead of being contradictory, enter and feel your teen's belief system and take an encouraging step instead of demeaning their viewpoint. If you acknowledge the intensity of the situation, you can successfully help your anxious teen. Validate their thoughts by telling them they can do it and handle the situation with courage, just like they did it in the past.

Stop Worrying, Or There's Nothing to Be Scared Of

Telling someone not to be worried when they are constantly exposed to worrying thoughts is unfitting and unreasonable. It's like putting a tiny bandage on a huge wound that is oozing pools of blood - in other words, it is useless and even demeaning in some cases. This form of reassurance can produce negative repercussions. Telling them not to be afraid of the future and incoming negative thoughts is useless and counter-intuitive. Since they have several fears, namely peer pressure, judgment, failure, not getting accepted, etc., telling them not to be afraid is meaningless. Instead, ask them what they fear the most and be open about confronting them. Instead of telling them "Don't worry" or "Stop worrying," ask them more about the nature of their worries and what you can do to cure them.

I Feel Anxious Too

Don't try to relate and compare your situation with your child's condition. Even though you may be trying to calm them down by portraying your example and telling them everything will be okay, they may perceive it negatively. By pressing on your anxiety, you are unknowingly belittling their serious condition. If you, as a parent, aren't taking it seriously, your child will lose all hopes of overcoming the situation, too. Even though you may feel anxious, you should not convey it to your teen. As an adult, you have a better sense of control and maturity to handle stress and deploy effective coping mechanisms. However, your teenage daughter or son is still immature and trying to learn several things simultaneously. Comparing your anxiety with your child's is far from unacceptable. Moreover, stress and anxiety can be contagious, and you should never feed off each other's anxiety.

You'll Be Fine

Telling them that they will be fine when they are clearly in a loop can be dangerous, too. Ignoring their heightened symptoms and shadowing them with a "You'll be fine" statement is a blatant lie. Your teen knows the true definition of "fine" is something that is way beyond their current situation and seems absurd. They believe that feeling fine is an overstatement, and they will never get to experience it. With a mind buzzing with thoughts and emotions and a heart that is constantly racing, your child will feel anything but fine. Your teen will not be fine until you take the matter seriously and take the necessary steps to treat them. Instead of saying that they will be fine, tell your troubled teen you will be there for them and help them with whatever they need.

I'll Do It for You

Since most anxious teens keep putting off things and delaying tasks, step in to encourage them to finish their chores instead of doing it for them. It can turn into a habit in the long run, and your teen may start relying on you to complete the smallest tasks that they could have managed. Let them gather their thoughts and find the courage and enthusiasm to finish the pending tasks on their own. By doing so, you will give them enough space to face reality and motivate them to be independent. Even though most anxious teens wish to address their thoughts, adamant parents who want to fix things for their teens at the earliest will get in the way. It often leads to parents saying things like, "You can rest. I will finish it for you." If you make this a habit, your teen will fail to acknowledge the tasks they are loaded with, leading to deeper procrastination and eventually affecting their grades and sense of responsibility.

You Need More Sleep

Many people with anxiety often resort to sleep as a coping mechanism. However, some may find it extremely difficult to sleep. They are constantly cited with anxious thoughts and negative emotions, leading to sleeping issues, other mental health issues, and even insomnia. Your teen may divert their anxiety and racing thoughts during the day by completing schoolwork or house chores. However, as the sun sets and the daily chaos submerges, their mind starts filling with worried thoughts about the future and the fear of failure making it difficult to sleep and causing restlessness. If all problems could be cured by sleep, everyone would be happy and carefree. You cannot tell them to sleep more if they cannot get even two to three hours of sleep in the first place. Instead, make them feel relaxed and suggest activities that induce sleep, such as meditation and aromatherapy.

Stop Thinking

Your anxious teen will not stop thinking if you simply ask them not to. Who wouldn't love to shut their racing thoughts and feel more relaxed? Naturally, it is not in their hands to stop thinking or worrying just because you mentioned it. Your teen may be caught up in a loop of negative and fearful thoughts, which are often difficult to overcome. If you cannot provide proper support, you won't break your child's thought cycle. Instead of asking your child to stop thinking, feed their brain with positivity and encouraging thoughts to balance out the negativity. Fill their mind with positive emotions to help them cope with the stressful thought process they are caught in. For example, if they are worried about failing their exams, do not tell them to shun such negative thoughts. Instead, motivate them by telling them how capable they are. Statements like, "You're worthy of achieving success" and "You can get into the college of your dreams" are some examples of positive reinforcement that your child needs to hear in their state of commotion.

Can You Hurry Up?

Asking them to hurry up or just complete a task without causing a fuss is off the charts. Teens diagnosed with chronic anxiety are often burdened with poor decision-making skills and regretting their past decisions. Some even try to achieve perfection in everything they do, which slows their pace. If you ask them to do things faster or hurry up, they will either mess up their tasks or feel guiltier. Since they are already feeling helpless and fear being judged, they will resent their presence and the way they handle things. Instead of pressurizing them to move hastily, ask them if you can do anything to help. Since they are prone to feeling panicky and anxious when doing certain things, like boarding a plane or being in a crowded place, give them time to overcome their fears and gather their thoughts. With your support, they can steadily increase their pace with time. Until then, try to be as patient as possible.

It's In Your Head

This is another statement that you should never utter in front of your anxious teen. These words are not only hurtful for your child but also represent your ignorant attitude. In a way, you are shaming your child by failing to acknowledge the real problem and blaming it on their brain. With time, your child will spiral into deeper pools of guilt and shame, after which pulling them out will be nearly impossible. Remember, your teen hasn't chosen to be in this state. If they could, they would have beaten this plight long ago. They still can if they have your support and the right insights to treat their condition. Word your sentences carefully when dealing with such situations. For example, a statement like, "Your worried brain is hyperactive and needs some rest. Why don't we get some ice cream and discuss your thoughts on our way?" can be very effective.

I Don't Understand What You Need

Supervising and taking care of an anxious teen can be confusing and exhausting. At times, you may not know what they want and why they behave in a certain way. It can be even more frustrating when your child is unwilling to talk to you and throws tantrums as a coping mechanism. However, you cannot take it out on your child. Even if you don't understand what your teen needs, you should not convey your ambiguity. Instead, talk to them and understand their thought process. Deep down, your child wants you to be supportive, patient, and calm, especially when they are hyperactive and caught in a loop. By displaying feelings of confusion and hopelessness, your child will feel even more lost and nervous. If you, as a parent, portray signs of failure, what is your child supposed to do?

Key Takeaway: Even though you may feel that you are a well-meaning and attentive parent, you may accidentally utter certain statements that heighten the negative anxiety symptoms in your teen instead of mellowing them down. Yes, it is difficult for you to see your child in their worst condition, but you shouldn't lose hope. Be supportive, say the right things, and provide the assurance of always being there for your child. Do not verbalize negative thoughts. Instead, learn the right way to deal with such intense situations. At times, listening to them with an open mind instead of uttering words of encouragement is more helpful. It also diminishes the chances of saying something unacceptable by accident. More importantly, every parent should stay calm and be affirmative to keep their child reassured.

CHAPTER 7

STRATEGIES TO SUPPORT AN ANXIOUS TEEN

By this point in the book, you have probably grasped a better idea of your teen's anxiety and understand that supporting them will not be a walk in the park. Before you try to help them, you must be fully aware that anxiety is highly unpredictable. You should also anticipate that the healing process will not be quick or predictable. It will usually feel like you and the child that you want to help are trying to navigate through a raging sea. No matter how understanding and compassionate they are, many parents who are determined to help their anxious children can easily lose their temper. Dealing with anxiety, more often than not, is a very frustrating experience for anyone involved. Regardless of how hard they try, no one who has never suffered from anxiety can wrap their head around the reality of this disorder. Many people tend to underestimate anxiety and its symptoms, although they may know a lot about how it works.

To most people, anxiety is a sign of weakness and is a reflection of a person's resilience, courage, and character. However, this couldn't be further from the truth. At first glance, anxiety seems like worry and fear of certain situations, and while this is true to an extent, it barely scratches the surface of anxiety. People who have anxiety are among the strongest people, and they regularly encounter and push themselves to the limit in various situations where they feel uncomfortable and anxious. You may get the idea that anxious teens are baffled and lost, though they are usually the first to come up with a practical solution in times of danger. The chances are that they have lived through numerous variations of the same situation in their minds and identified the different outcomes. Anxiety can set off at any given moment, without any warning. It doesn't mean there is something wrong going on in their brain. It simply means that your anxious teen's brain is a little more overprotective or preoccupied. Anxiety doesn't define your child, nor is it a personality trait. It is a wave of intense emotions that comes and goes.

Anxious brains are very strong and can feel impossible to fight against. They are persuasive and pervasive, and they will leave your child with negative thoughts and excessive worry. Its strength can trigger other disorders, such as OCD and panic disorders. Anxiety will leave your child feeling out of control, isolated, worried, afraid, and overwhelmed. It also comes with numerous physical symptoms, including nausea, tense muscles, tightness in the chest, and dizziness. It is often exhibited in behavioral symptoms like nail-biting and hair and skin picking. Anxiety is a very difficult battle to take on. Therefore, this book discusses strategies in detail to help you support an anxious teen.

Set Realistic Expectations

Setting Expectations

One of the most important things to do when you decide to jump right in and support an anxious teen is to set clear and realistic expectations. As discussed above, anxiety- whether it's at its peak or controlled is very mysterious. Regardless of whether you aim to help a teen entirely recover from their anxiety or just wish to help them fight the occasional battle, it will not be a smooth ride. Anticipating the best is very easy, especially when you are close to the child you're trying to help. It may be because you believe that you can help them, expect to get to them faster, presume that they are willing to accept your help or respond to your support, or simply wish to believe that they will feel better soon. However, approaching the situation with nothing but positivity can set you up for disappointment, but you both under more pressure, leave your teen feeling guilty, and make you feel bad for being unable to help them. You must remember that for your support to work, the effort needs to be twoway. They need to be fully willing to accept your help and not succumb to their anxiety. It's good to hope for the best, and it is recommended that you do so but don't set very high expectations. There are also times where you will feel like you are doing better, but don't get ahead of yourself and remember that it's not all sunshine and rainbows.

Don't Make It Personal

Understandably, you want your teen to defeat their anxiety and fears. Many parents believe that their children are capable of achieving so much and that anxiety is holding them back from unlocking their full potential. However, sharing those beliefs with someone with anxiety makes things worse for them. Pushing them to fight harder and imposing your help can be very distressing. Forcing a teen to face specific situations before they're ready is very counterproductive, leading to more psychological problems. You must prepare yourself for the worst as they may not feel prepared just yet, and may not even accept your support, to begin with. It doesn't mean that you should give up on them, and don't take their rejection personally either. You have to constantly remind yourself that the entire situation is not about you. These are not your fears, you are not the one facing them, and it is not up to you to decide when and how their anxiety should be tackled. You are a support figure - you are helping your teen out of love and compassion. It is not a mission - you are dealing with vulnerable human emotions. You merely need to be patient, listen to them, and take it at their pace.

Accepting Help

Being there for your teen even when they are not the easiest to deal with will eventually lead them to open up to you and give in to your support. People with anxiety don't choose how they feel, and even their rejection of your support can be a product of their anxiety. It's not easy for them to accept or ask for help. The thoughts and feelings accompanied by anxiety sometimes feel too personal. Other emotions and thoughts may be extremely intense, to the point where they feel terrified to explore. Many teens who have anxiety also deliberately associate it with their identity. They may feel afraid to explore who they are without the anxiety factor. These are all things that may cause them to push you away and capitulate to their anxiety.

What Are You Avoiding?

Supporting someone with anxiety is very tricky. If you've never been in the situation, you won't truly be able to tell what your anxious teen would and wouldn't like to hear. There are many phrases or words that you may think are reassuring and helpful, but in reality, they undervalue an anxious person's emotions and make them feel misunderstood. On the other hand, there are several things you may feel like you should avoid doing or saying when they are actually very helpful.

Discussing Thoughts and Emotions

Many people avoid talking about an anxious teen's emotions and focus on making them laugh or lighten up the mood instead. When dealing with an anxious child, don't avoid discussing their thoughts and feelings. Emotions and ideas are the core of anxiety - when you don't tackle the main issue, it may seem like you would rather do something more fun rather than listening to the child. While you may be doing this purely out of good intentions, your teen may feel like they are burdensome or boring. It will prevent them from discussing their worries with you in the future. Besides, a good laugh is a temporary fix. Meanwhile, delving into the main problem helps your teen gain clarity and helping them when they're in similar situations.

Encouraging Therapy

You may think that encouraging therapy or supporting them to seek professional help is insulting. You may be surprised to learn that many teens with psychological disorders wish to have someone willing to support them throughout this journey. Many teens wish to seek professional support but are afraid. If you change the subject when they bring up therapy or reluctantly talk about it, you may be unintentionally encouraging the stigma. Don't push them to see a therapist, but instead, ask them how they feel about seeing one. Explain to them why you think this may be a good idea and offer to help them find a professional with whom they feel comfortable. Offer to go with them and stay in the waiting room until they finish. If they feel overwhelmed, ask if they would like you to help them plan what they want to talk to the therapist about. Don't make them feel like they need to tell you what went on during the session, as they will tell you if they feel comfortable enough.

Looking After Yourself

Helping someone with a mental illness is a great challenge, and just like you may feel the need to look after them, you must look after yourself. You may tell yourself that now is not the time to make time for yourself or that they need your help more than you need looking after. However, you need to remember that overloading yourself affects your mental health, too. Keep in mind that no matter the type of relationship you have with your teen, you are not responsible for diminishing their anxiety. Besides, you have to help yourself before you can help them. Only focusing on the anxious adolescent will eventually make you unable to support them, in the same way, any longer. If you notice that you have started feeling unwell, it is time to set boundaries. Determine how much help you can offer and your limits. If possible, have someone else support them during the process so that not all of the weight falls on you. As long as you don't share with others information about your teen's issues, you are allowed to talk to others about how you are feeling. You need the support as well.

Worrying Isn't Bad

As someone who is deeply involved in anxiety's complexities, you can be led to believe that "worry" is a nemesis. This belief can be very harmful to you and the child you are trying to help. Believing that worrying, in general, is a bad thing causes problems for you later on. It also promotes toxic positivity, making you feel like you need to force a positive mindset even when things get very hard. There is a difference between excessive worry and obsessing over the tiniest details to the point of an anxiety disorder and worrying in alarming or drastic situations. People with anxiety disorders worry about things as simple as walking over to the garbage can during a meeting or class. They will replay the situation several times in their mind and think about multiple ways of how this scenario can play out. Worrying to this extent is unhealthy. However, worrying is a normal human function and is what makes us human. If you don't worry, you will not develop a defense strategy or trigger a fight or flight response in dangerous situations. If you don't worry about your health, you won't maintain healthy habits. If you don't worry about relationships, you will not make an effort to maintain them and end up losing many friends - the list goes on. This is what you should explain to your child precisely. Make it clear that you are trying to combat unhealthy worry and not worry as a concept.

Anxiety Coping Kit

Anxiety is like a ticking time bomb. It can go off anywhere at any time. Meaning, that no matter how close you are to the teen with anxiety, you can't guarantee that you'll be there every time they feel anxious. Even if you are worried for them, you can't constantly monitor or accompany them wherever they go. However, it's always good to be prepared. There are many ways to deal with anxiety, and creating an anxiety coping kit is one of them. An anxiety coping kit is a collection of various physical items, activities, notes, and reminders. Since each teen experiences anxiety differently, offer to create their coping kit with them or gather as much information about their thoughts, feelings, symptoms, and behavior when their anxiety kicks in before creating it for them.

An effective anxiety coping kit can include a written note that reminds them to take 10 deep breaths as this helps ease hyperventilation and shortness of breath. A note that reminds them to use the 54321 grounding technique will also be of great help. Ask them to name 5 things they can see, think of 4 things they can feel on their body, listen to 3 sounds, name 2 things they can smell, and 1 thing they can taste. If they have a prescribed inhaler for their panic or anxiety attacks, ensure to include it in the kit. Many teens experience digestive issues or loss of appetite with their anxiety, so include their favorite snack bar or a protein shake to ensure they still get healthy nutrition. Include a small notebook and a pencil since writing their feelings down helps them gain insight and express their emotions. If your teen sees a therapist, encourage them to take the notebook with them to their following session. A note with a list of names and contact numbers of people they can reach out to is important to include as hearing a loved one's voice can be very soothing. Make sure to include a small activity, such as an adult coloring book, a fidget toy or cube, or a Rubik's cube, to keep them occupied. This prevents them from exhibiting harmful behavioral symptoms. Write a letter to your child, or ask them to write a letter to themself and include it in the kit. The letter can be a list of things they're good at, things they're passionate about, and what they love about themselves, their affirmations, or even a reminder that their current situation is temporary. Though it is not portable, a weighted blanket helps soothe their anxiety if they're at home. It will make them feel guarded, secure, and safe. Add a funny memory or picture to give them something to smile about. Laughter can lower your teen's cortisol levels, which are responsible for stress hormones. Ask them to write down their blessings or things they're grateful for and include the note in the kit.

Reframing Anxious Thoughts

Reframing anxiety is a process that allows anxious teens to reinterpret an experience, situation, or event. This technique allows them to change the way they perceive something and, therefore, change how they feel about it. Reframing can help them overcome their anxiety and is completed through a simple process. The next time your teen feels anxious, ask them to write down the problem or situation, followed by their thoughts regarding it. Then, ask them to write down how they feel about it. Afterward, the reformation process begins. Ask them to write 4 alternative thoughts to the situation. For instance, if they're worried about trying out a new sport, the alternative thoughts could look like the following: if they ended up hating it, at least they found out how they feel about it, or if they liked it, but it's painful, then they are strengthening their muscles. The next step is listing evidence that supports the alternative thoughts they created. This can be personal evidence, such as evidence of personal growth. The final step is writing down how they feel after reframing their thoughts.

Practice Empathy

One of the most important things to do if you want to support your teen with anxiety is to practice empathy. You probably already feel compassion for them. However, many parents forget to express these feelings. It is important to stay strong for them and approach the situation strategically, though sometimes they prefer to know that someone understands how they feel. Instead of constantly providing them with solutions, practice making them feel validated and express concern.

Concentrate On the Basics

Anxiety is not easy to deal with, and you might feel like you have to resort to complicated and drastic measures immediately. However, keep in mind that there is usually not much to do for your teen during the attack. Try to calm them down and ensure they feel safe. Practice breathing exercises with them, and once they start feeling better, you can start to explore their thoughts and feelings with them. Let them know that you are there for them, understand them, and want to help them.

Key Takeaway: Supporting a teen with anxiety may be one of the hardest things you'll ever have to do. Anxiety is a very complicated mental disorder. It constantly eats away at the teen's mind and may even cause them to reject help even when they need it. To help someone manage their anxiety, you must truly understand how they feel and how their thoughts are tied to these emotions. It's helpful to explore different coping techniques to find out which method is most effective. As long as you don't pressure them or overload yourself at the expense of supporting them, progress can be made.

CHAPTER 8

SELF-SOOTHING TECHNIQUES FOR TEENS WITH ANXIETY

As discussed in the previous chapters, anxiety in the teenage years can be quite severe. While seeing a therapist can guide teens in the right direction, there are also plenty of exercises and techniques they can practice on their own to become mindful and to anchor themselves in the present moment. Self-soothing techniques should never be used as a cure but as a means to control thoughts in the conscious mind, and with time, train the subconscious to see the bigger picture. These techniques are recommended by certified psychotherapists and have proven to be an effective method to calm the mind and work on "resetting" the brain. This chapter covers the practices to help teens reduce stress and soften any feelings of anxiety that would otherwise snowball into a panic attack.

Practices for Long-term Effects

Acceptance

While it may sound counterproductive, psychotherapists advise teens to accept their anxiety as a selfpreservative knee-jerk reaction to stressful situations. Anxiety is more understood as a disorder in this day and age, and teens must understand that there is no shame in their struggle and that they're not alone.

Feelings of anxiety can either be inherited, the result of a rough upbringing, or past traumas – but whatever the cause, its function is to signal the individual that they're in a state of danger. It can be a danger of failing, losing someone dear to them, or perceived belittlement or embarrassment. As mentioned in previous chapters, anxiety in teens can also be fueled by bullying at school or poor self-esteem. Accepting the cause and the outcome is the first step to treatment.

Psychotherapists claim that any attempt of suppressing shame will backfire and worsen anxiety. Therefore, it's advised for anxious teens to see a therapist regularly so that they can pinpoint any potential causes of their worries and work on resolving or accepting them.

Yoga for Mindfulness

An anxious mind wanders to the past or gets caught in a web of possible future scenarios, and working on anchoring oneself in the present moment is a crucial step toward a calmer mind, which is known as a state of mindfulness. Unfortunately, neurodivergent teens with attention disorders may find this practice more challenging than others, but it's not a challenge that they cannot overcome with dedication and support.

Teens can tell their Yoga instructors specifically why they're taking up the practice. This way, yoga poses that directly ease feelings of anxiety can be taught from the beginning. These poses include but are not limited to the tree pose, the extended triangle pose, the child's pose, the half-moon pose, the bridge pose, among others. Specific poses can easily be learned online, as they are quite easy to do and require nothing but a yoga mat.

Aerobic Exercise

Although an active lifestyle should never be seen as the ultimate replacement for prescribed medication, countless studies prove the benefits of aerobic exercise in helping individuals manage common anxiety symptoms.

Traditionally, it was presumed that active lifestyles lead to a more positive body image and making individuals more confident. However, modern studies suggest that only five minutes of aerobic exercise per day can stimulate anti-anxiety effects. Some of these studies state that five to ten minutes is as effective as an intense 45-minute workout session.

When teens exercise, their bodies release "happy" hormones and chemicals, such as dopamine and other endorphins that stabilize the mood and regulate other hormones like serotonin. This not only impacts a teen's mood but also enables their brain cells to become more "active."

To reap the benefits of exercise, teens can go for a morning jog, do cardio at home, or get an exercise companion and go to the gym as part of a daily routine.

Tai Chi

Also known as shadowboxing, Tai Chi is a Chinese martial art form commonly practiced for self-defense. However, it also incorporates mindfulness and meditation, making it a physical and a mental exercise. It is one of the most highly recommended practices for those who have anxiety.

Due to the nature of Tai Chi's relaxed and gentle motions, it effectively keeps stress at bay. Teens can sign up for classes online or at a martial art center. It's best to avoid free videos, as this form of martial arts is very particular and needs to be learned correctly and frequently performed to reap its myriad benefits.

Professional Tai Chi instructors teach breathing techniques and specific positions. Injuries are always a possibility if practiced incorrectly, so professional training is recommended.

Other benefits of Tai Chi include easing symptoms of depression, stabilizing the mood and preventing mood swings, increased stamina, better sleep quality, and reduced risk of joint pain, falls, and even heart failure.

Deep Breathing

Deep breathing is a relatively simple and easy exercise to learn. It effectively combats anxiety and panic attacks, and the outcome is almost instantaneous. The exercise works by lengthening the exhale rather than the inhale. The teen doesn't need to fill their lungs with air completely as long as they inhale a deep breath and take their time letting the air out through their noses.

The trick is to work on belly breathing - lie down with one hand on the chest and the other on their torso, right above the belly button. They must then breathe in through the nose for three seconds, noticing how their belly rises as the lungs fill with air, and breathe out through the mouth very slowly for around six seconds. They need to repeat this exercise for at least ten minutes, as this trains the muscles to breathe in deeper, which has immediate and longterm anti-anxiety effects.

Writing

Having a hobby helps teens relieve their overwhelming and worrying feelings by using an outlet to expend their negative and intrusive thoughts. Writing is a great exercise that helps teens pinpoint the root cause of their negative feelings. Whenever they find themselves in an anxious state, they can grab a pen and paper or use an electronic device to jot down what's on their minds.

While the exercise helps teens privately vent to themselves, writing in and of itself also allows the mind to focus on the act of writing rather than negative thoughts. This can last anywhere from a few minutes to an hour, and teens are advised to stop only when their anxiety has subsided.

It's best to designate time as part of a daily schedule to write. Incorporating this practice into routines trains the brain to identify problems and resolve them. Teens can present their writing to their therapist or legal guardian to help address their worries in a more practical approach and avoid these worries as potential panic triggers.

Art Therapy

Many types of art therapy are suitable for easing anxiety in teens. As previously discussed, having a hobby helps alleviate and soften symptoms. Studies have shown that these three types of art therapy are ideal for teens with anxiety disorders.

Slow Drawing

The teen doesn't need to be naturally good at drawing to take it up as a hobby. It's a skill that can be learned with time. Slow drawing, in particular, has shown promising results in easing feelings of worry as it's considered a meditative exercise. All the teen needs to slow-draw is a pencil and paper. The hand is moved at a slower pace than usual, which allows the teen to focus on nothing but the process they are performing. They can draw shapes, people, or even symbols of what's on their minds. This exercise can immediately calm the mind and clear all the negative thoughts.

Painting

Painting is hailed as an effective stress-reliever. Unlike slow painting, there is no particular technique that distinguishes it from painting as a leisure activity. Scientists believe that only 45 minutes of painting a day can boost a teen's confidence and keep anxiousness at bay.

Teens can sign up for painting classes or look for free online lessons. As an exercise, painting allows the teen to immerse themselves in the craft completely and focus on nothing but the piece they're working on. Studies also suggest that painting stimulates feel-good hormones like dopamine, potentially balancing a teen's brain chemicals, altering their behavior, thinking patterns, and reactions to different stimuli.

Clay Modeling

What makes working with clay the perfect exercise for neurodivergent teens is its sensory benefits. With nothing but clay and their hands, teens get more in touch with their movements and bodies as they use their fingers to create art. Because it's a form of art that requires patience to master, this trains a teen's brain to "slow down" and, in turn, makes them less fidgety and much calmer with time.

Techniques for Immediate Relief

While the previous exercises work on long-term results, there are quick practices that provide immediate calming effects that come in handy when the teen is on the brink of a panic or anxiety attack. These techniques can be practiced anywhere in public, but they most effectively provide relief when done in a quiet and comfortable space. An anxiety attack can be best described as a wave. Teens can guide their thoughts to a safe space until the wave passes. It's recommended they find a place where they can be alone for a few minutes before doing these exercises.

Counting

It sounds like a very simplistic exercise, and it is. Counting is an easy and effective way to give the mind something to focus on other than feelings and thoughts of anxiety. Counting exercises are helpful for neurodivergent teens with autism or ADHD who find themselves on the brink of a meltdown.

In this exercise, the teen closes their eyes and begins to count to ten slowly. If they're more anxious than usual, they can count to a higher number, but it's advised to stop and start over. The individual keeps counting to give the mind something else to focus on until anxious feelings subside. Because anxiety is more severe in some teens than others, this exercise can provide immediate relief or take a few minutes longer to work.

The trick is to focus on nothing but counting and avoid thinking about whether the exercise is working. If the teen is in a private space, they can combine this exercise with slow breathing techniques and visualization.

Moreover, while counting is best known to give immediate results, it also trains the brain to be redirected to a state of mindfulness when stress accumulates. With time, teens can find even quicker relief in a shorter period when practicing the exercise.

Confrontation

Confronting negative thoughts can be challenging. If the teen is not properly trained on how to do this, it can backfire, so it's important to practice this with a therapist or at home under supervision before they practice it on their own. Anxiety is, in most cases, exacerbated by other mental illnesses and disorders that can alter the negative thoughts that pass through the teen's mind, including harmful and untrue presumptions that add fuel to the fire. Confrontation is, therefore, a great tool to nip the cause in the bud and calm the mind with logic rather than by distracting it. This exercise is most effective when anxiety is still developing, and it should never be practiced in an attempt to dissuade a rapidly approaching panic attack.

The exercise works by breaking the cycle before it begins, and this is done by having a mental conversation with one's self. The teen starts by visualizing their anxious thoughts as a projected version of themselves – one that they can converse with and calm down, and they start asking questions of what it is that's worrying them. If the teen is in an overstimulating environment, such as a loud party or a large social gathering, they need to find a quiet and comfortable place before they begin.

If thoughts of anxiety are caused by a tight deadline at school, a social relationship, or any situation they don't have control over, they can ask themselves what the worst-case scenario would be and accept and make peace with it. For instance, if the consequence they're thinking of is failing a class, they can think of a reassuring backup plan, especially one that is previously devised with their parents' help. Therefore, it's important for parents and therapists to go over every detail that might be worrying the teen.

On the flip side, if the anxiety is rooted in something they cannot change, such as the death of a pet or loved one or moving, the teen needs to do the opposite of mindfulness. Instead of anchoring themselves in the present moment, they look ahead to the future and find peace in what is to come.

It's important to note that this is not an exercise that can be improvised. The answers to the questions that the teen asks themselves must be pre-determined with the help of a therapist or a legal guardian. This exercise helps organize their thoughts and reminds them of the bigger picture.

Correct Posture

Psychotherapy studies show a behavioral pattern in teens when they are anxious. When approaching a state of panic, instinct kicks in and leaves them in fight-or-flight mode, which usually makes them hunch over to protect the upper body – where the heart and lungs are, making it difficult to snap out of an anxious state.

If the teen finds themselves in this posture, they need to correct it immediately. They're advised to stand, straighten their backs, and pull back their shoulders and their feet planted on the ground firmly.

The next step is to close their eyes and breathe through their noses as deeply as possible until their lungs are full before exhaling through the mouth slowly. When the posture is combined with breathing exercises, the muscles become less tense, and the brain realizes that it's not in danger and that it's, most importantly, in full control. This, in turn, affects passing thoughts and calms the mind. It's also believed that posture correction softens anxiety and helps teens have firmer control over it.

Aromatherapy

In case a teen feels anxious in the comfort of their home, they can use aromatherapy for its soothing effects, sometimes in combination with the previous exercises for quicker relief. Essential oils are no magic cure, but studies have proven their efficacy in calming the body and mind and relieving stress. Lavender oil is the most popular choice for this technique, but teens can also use tea tree, basil, or citrus oils if they prefer a particular scent.

These oils can be used in a dispenser for long-term effects, or teens can carry a dropper with them. A few drops on the wrist and the neck can help, but essential oils are most effective when added to a warm bath, as this helps muscles relax and allows space to perform breathing exercises. The oils can also be massaged on the temples, or a few drops can be added to body lotion. This technique is not effective in an impending panic attack but rather in keeping stress at bay.

Herbal Teas

Before the advent of pharmaceuticals, herbs were used to treat anxiety and depression. Herbal teas have soothing effects, but they should never be used as a replacement for prescribed medication.

There's a range of herbs that teens can safely consume to reap their calming benefits. They're quick and easy to brew and can help anxious teens have better quality sleep, especially when anxiety causes insomnia. Peppermint leaves or peppermint extract can be consumed to relieve anxiety, while its scent is soothing and also used for aromatherapy.

Chamomile is another great herb that helps calm the mind and muscles, and it's also a powerful antiinflammatory. Because herbal teas have no caffeine content, there's practically no risk of overconsumption as long as refined sugar is not added. Studies suggest that long-term consumption of chamomile extract helps individuals control moderate to severe anxiety symptoms. Similarly, lavender is also a mood stabilizer and has sedative effects.

Another herb that can be consumed in tea is kava. It works by targeting GABA receptors, the part in the brain responsible for feelings of stress and worry. Although there's practically no risk of consuming these herbs, legal guardians should always consult the teen's physician before adding these natural remedies to their diets.

Audio Therapy

Music or audio therapy is a more experimental antianxiety technique. While it's scientifically proven that music releases endorphins and stabilizes moods, it's best used for short-term results and to relieve stress.

However, music therapy isn't simply having your teen listen to their favorite song. As suggested by anecdotal evidence, anti-anxiety audios, guided meditations, and so-called "subliminal" may provide immediate relief for some teens who struggle with frequent panic attacks.

Binaural beats and isochronic tones are usually embedded in these audio recordings. Usually categorized as "brainwave entrainment," these audio files contain two tones, each of a slightly different frequency. The small difference in the frequency is believed to trick the brain into hearing a third tone. It stimulates neurons in the brain to synchronize with this imaginary sound, which allegedly decreases anxiety and is even claimed to improve cognitive functions.

Some of these audio recordings that are barely audible may also embed positive affirmations in an attempt to bypass the conscious brain and plant these affirmations directly in the subconscious, which alters the teen's behavior over time. Although an experimental kind of therapy, some individuals report feeling more at ease overnight after listening to this music.

Key Takeaway: It's recommended to allow teens to choose the techniques and practices they're comfortable doing and to only follow up with their progress without pressuring them into doing more than what they have the energy for. Following several or all of the self-soothing techniques in this chapter will facilitate all areas of life, and not only a teen's state of mind. It's essential to stay consistent and to remember that results are accumulative and take time to show.

Psychotherapists recommend these practices, and if no significant progress is seen in a few weeks, parents must consult a certified psychotherapist who specializes in teen psychology.

CHAPTER 9

TEENAGE SUICIDE

Taking one's own life is an extremely strenuous decision, which is taken after a person develops a thought pattern compelling them to cause harm and end their life. When a teen is willing to undergo a process or experience that is dangerous to them and causes physical harm, the phenomenon is known as suicidal ideation, and this is often accompanied by suicidal behavior and relevant pathogenesis.

If your teen seems to be at risk of committing suicide, you must take immediate action to combat the situation and prevent them from causing self-harm.

Teens at Risk

Teens Who Have Been through Trauma

Trauma is the most common cause or sign of risk in teens who have tried to commit suicide. While addiction and depression are the two main triggers that compel teens to commit suicide, traumatic experiences are also a major reason that put them at risk. PostTraumatic Stress Disorder (PTSD) and Acute Stress Disorder (ASD) are the two common types of mental health issues that arise from trauma. Childhood trauma can steadily turn into ASD if left untreated for a prolonged period. It can be a violent incident, a horrifying accident, or the unexpected death of a loved one. Signs related to traumatization must be recognized at an early stage as teens are at a higher risk of committing suicide or hurting themselves.

Suicide History

If your family has a history of suicide, your teen may be at risk. The situation can be specifically intense if your child has witnessed someone committing suicide. Whether it's deliberate self-harm or a suicidal attempt, the young minds are easily influenced and vulnerable to committing suicide themselves. Since they are looking for an easy way to solve their issues, harming themselves becomes an easier option if they've witnessed a similar phenomenon. Instead of understanding the real cause and the severity of the situation, they take this intense step without seeking treatment. Several environmental conditions impulsivity also contribute to this condition and increase the chances of familial suicide, which means that both genetic impulses and non-genetic behavioral aspects may be passed on to the next generation. Pay specific attention to your teen's anxiety disorder if your family has been through a similar tragedy.

Substance Abuse

As you learned by now, excessive alcohol and drug use can lead to addiction. Since teens are not entirely mature and cannot control the amount of substance they consume, they often cross the line and dwindle into addiction. The use of substances is, directly and indirectly, related to self-destructive behaviors. Substance abuse paired with depression can enhance the intensity of your teen's suicidal mindset and put them in distress until they take a dangerous step. With time, the situation can worsen and lead to suicide. Drugs like lysergic acid diethylamide (LSD) and certain prescribed medications also increase the risk of overdose. In some countries, a lower age limit for drinking also affects teenagers' mindset. In most cases, teens and tweens aged 17 to 20 are more prone to developing suicidal thoughts due to the delicate drinking age limit. Let's not forget how easily teens are influenced by the people around them.

Signs of Depression

Among all reasons, depression is the number one reason that leads not only teens but also adults into practicing self-destructive behaviors. Depression is linked to anxiety, which can steadily take the suicidal form. Even though the stimulus and effects are not apparent, the coherence can be decoded from the teen's reactions to challenges and circumstances in each step of their life. The fear of failure or not being good enough can trigger depression, and the easiest way to cope is by ending their life. In a few cases, teens have steadily developed symptoms due to the comparison between various classes based on their social status, looks, and popularity. Any painful or demoting emotion is easily translated as the end of one's life, which is why teens lose the meaning of living and resort to self-harm.

Exposure to Physical or Sexual Violence

Bullying is one form of physical offense that your teen may be exposed to in school or neighborhood. It often boils down to family-related abuse and domestic violence. A teen exposed to violence, directly or indirectly, as a child is highly prone to developing unpleasant thoughts that can lead to self-harm as a coping mechanism. Parents who are imprisoned or have a criminal record also affect the young minds. Even though the parents face some form of violence either from their partner or others, it can majorly affect their children. So, if you live in a violent household, neighborhood, or environment, pay attention to your teen's feelings and emotions as it significantly heightens their anxiety.

Issues with Sexual Orientation

If a teen cannot accept their sexual orientation or is too scared to open up to their parents and family members, they can be at risk of committing suicide. The fear of being judged by society and not being accepted by others is at the brink of most homosexual teenagers' minds. This phenomenon is widely known as sexual orientation discordance, which elevates the chances of conducting self-harm. However, parents must try to come to terms with their child's mindsets and be open about their choices. After all, it's your child who has to live their life, then why not be happy for them? Since it is arduous and confusing for teens to make peace with their sexual orientation, be more supportive and help them face their emotions instead of making it more difficult.

What to Look for in a Suicidal Teenager

The best way to save your teenager from committing suicide is to look for signs and taking immediate and effective steps to curtail them.

Constant Mood Swings

While teens commonly experience occasional mood swings, a consistent pattern can threaten their mental health. Rapid shifts in mood are also connected to severe issues, such as bipolar disorder, which can increase suicidal tendencies. While being happy or sad at occasional intervals is acceptable, it should be taken seriously if it interferes with their lifestyle quality. If your teen is portraying signs of mood swings that seem difficult to control, seek help from professionals to get to the bottom of the issue. In most cases, substance abuse and hormonal changes are the two common causes. However, being extremely happy one day and lashing out at others on the next can take a toll on your teen's mental health. If you see your teen spending a lot of money when they are happy and feel like harming themselves when they are in a bad mood, these are signs of mood swings that can lead to suicide.

Feeling Hopeless

If your teen is displaying signs of hopelessness and unable to perceive a future, they are also at a higher risk. Feeling hopeless is often related to a chemical imbalance that is difficult to diagnose at an early stage. When combined with the feeling of not being appreciated by their loved ones or rejected by their crush can enhance the emotion of despair they are already facing. The angst is also often shadowed by humiliation and shame. Repetition in behavior, seeking perfection to cover up their guilt, and feeling hopeless or hesitant speech are often accompanying signs.

Making Suicidal Statements

Statements like "I feel like dying," "I wish to end my life," or "Death seems to be the easiest answer to all these problems" are some direct verbal cues that clearly state a teen's motive. They may even be seen carrying or holding dangerous objects or looking for strategies to harm themselves. It is believed that most teens who constantly make suicidal statements are crying for help. It may seem that your teen is threatening you by narrating instances and statements related to suicide, but it can be much more serious and intimidating than you imagine. Most parents ignore these statements considering them to be attentionseeking. Do not make the same mistake as the adolescents who fail to get help and are often subjects of suicide.

Staying Isolated

Teenagers who prefer to be alone can steadily develop the mindset of harming themselves. Even if their loved ones are trying to reach them, they somehow feel that they are and will remain alone for the rest of their lives, and this makes the act of committing suicide easier. When they are alone, the risk of self-harm increases as there is no one to monitor or stop them, which is why parents must be more careful when their teens prefer to stay alone most of the time. It is known that loneliness and social isolation are as dangerous as smoking 15 cigarettes a day. Along with cognitive decline, rising physical and mental health issues, impaired immunity, and lack of sleep, most teenagers exposed to suicidal ideation are compelled to harm themselves.

Previous Attempts at Self-Harm

Teens who have tried to harm themselves in the past are undeniably at a higher risk of taking their lives. Parents must closely monitor their condition and pay attention to their behavioral pattern at all stages. However, just because they have displayed a previous attempt at suicide does not mean that the risk of reattempt will increase. If your teen is provided optimum attention and care, the symptoms can be treated with time. For instance, a simple intervention program held by the guardian or an expert will gain insights into the teen's chances of reattempting suicide.

Changes in Personality and Attitude

This also often stems from the symptoms and aftereffects of depression. Teens and tweens suffering from depression will be caught portraying changes in their personality and behavior. They may either seem quieter or become meaner. You may even catch them giving away their belongings to others or parting ways with the possessions they valued.

Diagnosis

Physical and Mental Health Diagnosis

The first and most important step of diagnosis is noticing and tracking physical and mental health deterioration signs. As mentioned in the previous chapters, individuals with combined signs of physical and mental issues are closely related to the emerging suicide ideation. Blood and urine tests are run to detect physical signs related to hormonal changes and genetic issues. Your teen may also undergo a thorough medical test under a psychiatrist to determine the triggers that compelled them to cause self-harm.

Type of Medication Prescribed

At times, teens undergoing medication may also get suicidal thoughts, so medical practitioners test the prescriptions and medicines they are taking. Paired with hormonal changes and mood swings, certain over-the-counter drugs are dangerous for young minds. Even though the cases are rare, many teens get suicidal feelings due to the medication they are prescribed.

Addiction

As mentioned, teens addicted to a varied range of substances are also diagnosed to determine if the substance use was the main cause of fathering their suicidal ideation. The tests will demonstrate if the teen suffered from damages due to alcohol and drug abuse and if they were the main reason behind the suicidal attempt. If they are even borderline addicted, the practitioner will provide medication and therapy to treat it. In extreme cases, they may be sent to a rehabilitation center to cure their addiction.

Treatment

Medication

Some medication reduces the signs of suicide and encourages your teen to look at the brighter side. Your teen's medical practitioner will prescribe antipsychotic medications, antidepressants, or medicines related to treat anti-anxiety, depending on their case.

Psychotherapy

This is probably the most effective way to treat suicide. Commonly known as talk therapy or psychological counseling, this form of treatment will dig deeper into your teen's emotions and help them cope with their fears. It also helps treat and diminish suicidal ideation.

How Can I Help Prevent Teen Suicide?

As we know, prevention is better than cure in all cases. Instead of treating and amending your teen's suicidal or self-harm, it is best to prevent it from happening in the first place. Failing to pay attention to your teen can push them in the wrong direction and elevate the chances of causing self-harm.

Reach Out to Your Teen

Instead of giving unwanted and undue criticism, listen to them with an open mind and ask if you can do anything to help. Be with them and mean it. Acknowledge their skills, presence, and talent. Tell them how capable they are of achieving anything they wish. Reach out for help and keep them hooked. In other words, make them feel appreciated.

Help Them Live a Healthy Lifestyle

Developing a healthy lifestyle by exercising and following a healthy diet are effective strategies to cope with mental health issues and reduce suicidal ideation. For this, you must incorporate some form of physical activity in your routines, such as a 30-min walk or attending a spin class. Plan your teen's diet and feed them healthy food to improve their physical and mental health. Take help from a medical practitioner or certified nutritionist to help you plan a diet based on your teen's mental health condition.

Keep Alcohol and Harmful Substances out of Reach

Needless to say, keep alcohol, drugs, and other addictive substances out of your teen's reach. They will be tempted to try out every kind of substance that is within their reach. Explain the negative repercussions of drinking alcohol and doing drugs to keep your teen away from such vices, preventing drug overdose or alcohol poisoning suicide. Since young adults are highly likely to commit suicide by popping multiple sleeping pills, ensure that they are kept away from such dangerous triggers.

Spend More Time with Them

The idea is to show your support as a parent and ward off the negative effects of social isolation. By spending time with them, they will be assured of having someone by their side who will listen and support them. Perform activities that your teen likes to do. Whether it's playing video games, shopping, or baking, do what they like when spending time with them. It keeps them distracted and happy. More importantly, they will feel like sharing their worries and fears with you as you get closer. Staying aligned with a teenager's mind is challenging, especially for parents, and encouraging them to spend time with you is the easiest way to break this barrier.

Support Them throughout Therapy

At times, just being with them can make a world of difference. Accompany your teen to their therapy sessions and ensure that they are comfortable throughout. Drive them to and from their sessions, especially if they are feeling nervous. If they cannot keep up, talk to their therapist to change their treatment and medication course.

When to Call a Doctor and How to Handle an Appointment

Even though you took preventive measures and paid attention to your teen, they may still end up harming themselves or attempting suicide. In an emergency, call your partner, family member, or someone close to you to get additional help, and, most importantly, call an emergency service. If you find out that your teen has already attempted suicide and is in a severe condition, call an emergency ambulance service and transfer them to a medical facility at the earliest. Make sure that they are tended to at the earliest to decrease the severity of their condition. The medical practitioner will conduct a thorough examination and look for physical signs of damage in your teen. They will also check for signs to decipher the causes that led your teen to commit suicide. Furthermore, they will also ask you questions related to your teen's previous suicide attempt, if any.

Depending on the severity of the case, your child will be admitted to the hospital to gain further treatment. You will remain at the hospital to supervise your child's condition to avoid a reattempt suicide. Do not feel hesitant to ask questions like, "Are you having thoughts of harming yourself?" and "Are you thinking of committing suicide?" They may sound extremely straightforward and downright pathological, but they help you figure out the severity of the situation. If your teen answers with a yes, immediately take help from the experts. While booking a doctor's appointment may take some time, in the meanwhile, get in touch with a crisis hotline. Most countries have urgent care clinics that take care of patients who have made suicidal attempts.

Lastly, be wary of the misconceptions related to anxiety and suicide. Since most people believe that suicide is solely based on personal decisions, the situation isn't taken as seriously as it should be. Furthermore, statements like, "There is no way out for people with suicidal thoughts" or "You should not talk with people about suicide as it can give them the idea" are completely wrong. In contrast, suicidal impulses are treatable if recognized early. Do not assume that by not talking about suicide, your teen will be safe and avoid causing self-harm.

Key Takeaway: Irrespective of how hopeless and worthless your teen might feel, proper attention and care will help them lead a healthy life both physically and mentally. Several cases of teens with suicidal intentions who now lead healthier lives are present today as proof. As a parent, your role is to recognize these tendencies and pull your teen out of danger at the earliest.

CHAPTER 10

PARENTING AND ANXIETY

When dealing with your teens' anxiety, you must be prepared to keep up and pull your teen out of this misery. As instructed on an airplane to wear oxygen masks before assisting others, consider a similar situation when helping your anxious teen. This chapter will take a look at some self-care tips for parents and how to deal with your anxiety to help your child in a better way.

Self-Care Tips for Parents

Consider these self-care tips for parents to control anxiety and take care of themselves to help their teens in despair.

Start Prioritizing

Prioritize your needs and tasks to stay on track and understand what is important and what can be discarded. It will also help you organize your schedule and map out your tasks based on your week. Parents are not superheroes who can work continuously without becoming exhausted. You are a human and get tired after working for long hours. Create a worklife balance by prioritizing your tasks and setting your obligations apart. Most of the time, priorities include spending time with your loved ones and family members. Share your priorities that seem like an obligation with your partner, making them easier to handle. With your partner's help, you can make difficult decisions with ease and fulfill them in a jiffy. Note that your priorities aren't your tasks, so they should not be perceived or treated as milestones or things on your to-do list. Your tasks that cannot be deemed as priorities should be taken off the list.

Take Some Time Out

As parents, you should take some time out for yourselves to rejuvenate and feel fresh. Working all week and fulfilling your duties takes a major toll on your physical and mental health. By taking some time out for yourself, you will take better care of your health and supervise your teen's condition with optimum diligence. Even if you cannot take an entire day or week off due to your busy schedule, take at least 20 to 30 minutes off in a day, preferably before bed. Use this time to relax, distress, and do what you love - read a book, lie down while listening to music, confront your thoughts, and get your head clear.

Spending Time with Your Loved Ones

Spend time with your children, partner, family members, and those you consider close every once in a while. Since humans are swamped in daily chores and obligations, they often forget to interact with others. Structure your time so that you see and spend time with your loved ones and your family. It is not only necessary for you as parents but also for your teenager. Host dinners and organize informal parties for your loved ones to stay in touch with each other. You can also organize a routine or design a ritual to spend time with your family after dinner. After dinner, playing a board game is a simple ritual that goes a long way in keeping your family united and close. Plan a game night with your loved ones or take cooking classes with your teen. Take your family out on a camping trip or hiking in nature, which helps treat your family's mental health issues, too.

Pamper Yourself

You have all the right to pamper yourself, and you completely deserve it. Do not feel guilty when taking a break and indulging in your favorite activities. Take a nap, read your favorite book, sip on a warm cup of tea, and light a scented candle. At times, simple pleasures like these can go a long way and make you appreciate life. Indulge in mindfulness practices, such as visiting a spa or taking a break and watching movies at home. Whether you have 10 minutes or an entire day, you can find ways to pamper yourself at home. For instance, if you have just 10 to 15 minutes to spare, wear a facial mask and meditate while listening to calming music. On the contrary, if you have the whole day free, take a nap, visit your favorite restaurant, or run a movie marathon.

Find Your Support System

While you need to take care of yourself to supervise your teen's condition, it's important to find yourself a caretaker or support system to lean on. You need your own caretaker to share your worries with and who can provide optimum assistance in times of despair. Even though you might have several people in your life, narrow down your options by considering the people who will help you in times of need. It can be your parents, best friend, or a well-wisher who will carefully listen to your thoughts and help you overcome them. Is there anyone you respect and go to for advice in distressing times? Sometimes, you don't want someone to listen but just be there for you and provide comfort as you face your fears.

Go Out

Whenever you get time, go out and celebrate the tiny milestones in your life. Whether it's going to a diner to grab a milkshake or going on a long road trip with your family, go out as much as you can. It will keep you excited and on your toes. Do not consider grocery shopping or running errands as going out. Be out in nature, go for a walk, or take your children to an amusement park. Spending time outside with your family will help you rekindle decaying relationships and reconstruct a new bond.

Organization Matters

While organizing your life and prioritizing your needs is of the utmost importance, also ensure that the environment you live in is organized. Being and living in a cluttered space is extremely off-putting and causes stress. It also makes finding essential things on time a lot more difficult. When decluttering your space, start by collecting and discarding things you don't use or won't use in the future. Do not get emotionally attached to your belongings. Let them go and give them away to people in need. With a clear space and environment, you will think clearly, too. For some people, cleaning and decluttering is a form of therapy. Try it for yourself, and you will feel at ease, too. If it seems too overwhelming, ask your family to help and turn it into a fun family activity.

By organization, we also mean organizing various other factors of your life. For instance, it can be managing your expenses and finances, scheduling time to prepare your meals and spend time with your family, and organizing your time to indulge in a self-care routine. Failing to organize your life will not only delay your chores but also keep you super busy. In such cases, forget about pampering yourself or taking time out to relax.

Concentrate On Your Future

Instead of cribbing about your past, divert all your attention towards making a better future. Whether it's the next day or the next five years, draft a rough idea to keep your goals in mind. If your main goal needs a lot of hard work and capital, start working on it today and saving money.

Your Health is Important

If you are unhealthy and keep getting sick, there is no hope for your child to stay robust. After all, you have to take care of their melancholy and treat it at the earliest. If you, the support system, fall ill, there is no one to take care of your teen. So, keep your health in check, making it a priority. Take care of your physical, mental, and emotional health as all three are necessary to stay active and think straight. A slight imbalance in this system can create havoc and worsen the situation.

Here is how you can take care of your physical health.

Exercise Regularly: Join a gym or take a spin class to keep your body in shape. Exercising helps you lose weight, maintains your physical health, and keeps your mental health in check. Since exercising is also known to balance your hormonal levels and secrete endorphins (the happy hormone), you will feel much more active and productive throughout the day. Encourage your teen and other family members to participate in some form of physical activity with you. Even if you cannot take some time out to exercise due to a busy schedule, try to squeeze in at least 30 minutes of walking throughout the day.

Design a Well-Balanced and Nutritious Diet: A balanced and nutritious diet is essential to provide the necessary nutrients to your body for optimum functioning and health. It will also help treat any existing health issues and prevent other problems from occurring. For instance, the risk of strokes, diabetes, osteoporosis, and some cancers can be lowered by designing a nutritious diet. Do not take the risk of designing a diet on your own. Consult a certified nutritionist to help you prepare a food chart based on your existing physical and health condition.

Drink Plenty of Water: Drink at least 8 to 10 glasses of water in a day. This is the minimum amount per day but the more, the better. It reduces stress levels and keeps you hydrated. Dehydration is the main cause of several health issues, such as migraine and kidney problems, so drinking more water keeps such issues at bay. Keep a water bottle or jug on your table to remind you to keep sipping on water throughout the day. You can also make lemonade or drink hot tea to complete your daily water intake.

Get 8 Hours of Sleep: Sleep is the solution to many health problems. Getting less sleep will not only affect your eyes and skin but also increase your stress levels. Lack of sleep can lead to drastic weight gain in a shorter period. Sleep and anxiety are closely interlinked, so you should focus on getting at least 7 to 8 hours of sound sleep every night. If you have trouble falling asleep, sip on chamomile tea and listen to peaceful music before going to bed. Once you train your body to sleep and wake up at a designated time, its circadian rhythms will adjust accordingly and help you sleep at the same time each night.

Here are some mindfulness practices to include in your regimen to improve your mental health and ward off your anxiety.

Visualization Techniques: These self-imagery techniques are known to treat anxiety, agoraphobia, and panic attacks due to their ability to calm your mind. They also help you get in touch with your true and unfiltered emotions, which eventually reduce anxiety symptoms and related disorders. One of the most effective ways to practice visualization techniques is by tuning into guided imagery. Close your eyes and lie down on a flat surface. Play calming music to concentrate and place your hands beside you. Imagine any scene or place that you love. It could be a beach, the woods, or the mountains. Take deep breaths and imagine being there as you slowly guide your imagination to explore the virtual place. Once you are fully immersed in your imagination, slowly open your eyes and notice how your mind and body feel. Practice this exercise daily, preferably when you feel super anxious.

Breathing Techniques: Since your breathing is often affected by anxiety, practice certain breathing exercises to alleviate the symptoms. This technique is super helpful during anxiety attacks and rapid breathing. While deep breathing and meditation help, you can also try abdomen and belly breathing techniques to feel calmer. Your one hand should rest on your chest and the other on your abdomen or belly. Inhale deeply and notice your belly rising as the air enters your body. Keep your stomach muscles engaged when exhaling through your mouth. Try resonate breathing or alternate nostril breathing techniques for a similar effect.

Journaling: Keep a diary or a journal and enlist your feelings and thoughts that you go through all day. Since journaling is an effective stress-buster and helps you cope with your fears, it is a sure-shot way to combat anxiety. It is also great for overall wellbeing and improving your emotional health. You can unleash your creativity and go limitless with how you journal. Use stickers, colorful pens, or any other creative tools to make journaling an enjoyable experience and a hobby you'd look forward to daily. Keep track of your eating habits, exercise regime, and any other tasks when journaling to improve your wellbeing.

Another way to feel at ease is by practicing gratitude every night before you go to bed. Mention three things you are grateful for and write them down in your diary. It can be anything as lucid as the food on your plate or as magnificent as your huge house. This might seem useless, but it does work in the long run. Knowing that you have something to be thankful for, you will feel happier and blessed, which means a great deal to your mental health.

With these practices, you can keep your senses in check and eliminate the chances of getting caught up in a loop of anxious thoughts, worries, and fears.

Get Yourself Checked

Schedule regular appointments at your doctor's clinic and get yourself checked every once in a while. Whether it's your general practitioner or your dentist, take care of your body and be aware of it by getting yourself checked once every 6 months. If needed, get your blood and urine tests to treat your nutrient deficiency and design a healthier diet.

Whether or not you suffer from anxiety or a related disorder, consider these self-care tips and make them a permanent part of your lifestyle as they will help you feel calmer and create a work-life balance.

Learn What Triggers You

You cannot treat your teen's anxiety if you fail to control your condition. If you can recognize signs that may seem like an anxiety disorder, get yourself checked and identify the triggers for better control. Instead of dwelling on your anxiety and worries, recognize what created them in the first place. Once you can identify the triggers, you can treat them effectively. By doing this homework, you will help your anxious teen, too. Merely because you feel a certain way does not necessarily mean that you have a serious health issue, so recognize the signs, become aware, and stay in tune with your body.

Once you know your triggers, you can easily set boundaries and keep them away to cope with the situation more sensibly. Learning what triggers you helps you design a treatment plan that effectively combats the situation and reduces symptoms. As mentioned, if you are calm, you can take care of your anxious teen too. While being stressed is a common phenomenon in most adults, it can become an issue if it turns into hypertension or anxiety. Therefore, learn about your triggers at the earliest.

Know-How to Combat Stress

Combating and managing stress becomes easier when you know what's causing it. While simple self-care tips are an effective way to cope with stress and feel at ease, suitable steps should be taken to tackle more intense situations. Consult a clinician or a therapist if your stress or anxiety seems unmanageable. Combating your stress is even more necessary as your teen replicates your behavior. If they see you effectively managing your stress and coping with your anxiety, they will model your behavior and take cues from you. This simultaneous process can efficiently scaffold your teen's way of managing stress and tolerating anxiety.

The breathing and mindfulness practices described above help alleviate anxiety and panic. If your situation seems intense, seek help from a medical practitioner and recognize your triggers to treat them more effectively. Once you know how to tolerate and ward off stress, teach your teen the same mannerisms and encourage them to take cues. The modeling behavior of children that we mentioned in previous chapters can help here. If your idea is to rationally think when feeling anxious, convey the same feeling and ask your teen relevant questions. For instance, calm your teen by conveying the exact emotions you feel when dealing with anxiety. A statement like, "Being scared is not uncommon, but what are the chances that you will face something so scary?" This can significantly help your child cope with their issue and feel calmer. Whether or not you are coping with your anxiety, always stay calm and composed in front of your child. Since your teens will model your behavior, your words, how you express your emotions, and the intensity of your facial expressions, you must be extra careful.

Key Takeaway: Before you learn about and treat your teen's anxiety, it is necessary to treat your anxiety disorder or any other form of mental illness first. It helps you cope with your child's condition and pull them out of this hole at the earliest. Once you can identify the triggers, take the necessary steps to treat them and alleviate anxiety. Consider the self-care tips taught in this chapter to create a work-life balance and cope with your anxiety. Spend some time out, do things you like, and take care of your health to build a strong support system and backbone for your teen.

CONCLUSION

While you may wish to turn back time and prevent the problem from occurring in the first place, we all know it is not impossible. The only thing you can do is look ahead and find a solution by digging deeper into the crux of the problem. Instead of cursing your younger self, look out for your teen and help them cope with their issues.

As mentioned throughout the book, treating chronic anxiety is extremely crucial, especially in teens, as it can deteriorate their quality of life and become a lifethreatening episode.

Let's summarize what we've learned so far to illustrate an overall picture. Start by understanding what anxiety is and whether or not it is normal. Since anxiety is more frequently detected in adults, teens and tweens' anxiety can seem overwhelming for parents. However, instead of panicking, understand if your teen actually has chronic anxiety. Next, narrow down the plausible causes that could have led to the moments of panic that your teen regularly goes through. At times, peer pressure, changing hormones, rising competition, and societal pressure are the main reasons. In other cases, parents unknowingly push their kids into a downward spiral that steadily gives birth to anxious thoughts.

Garner help from this book to recognize the exact signs and causes of teenage anxiety. Some effective treatment options based on your child's condition and the circumstance's severity are also mentioned. Next, know how to talk to your kid about anxiety and what not to say. Saying the wrong thing can trigger negative feelings and worsen the condition. Refer to the examples of phrases and statements mentioned in chapter 6 to put your child at ease. Assure your teen that you're with them and acting as a support system 24/7.

Deploy effective strategies to combat the situation, support your teen, and portray your expectations. You can also teach self-soothing techniques such as deep breathing, aerobic exercises, and mindfulness practices to ease the symptoms. If your teen has already been clinically diagnosed with chronic anxiety, keep an eye on them to prevent the development of suicidal ideation. Closely monitor the situation if they have previously attempted suicide or have harmed themselves.

Lastly, do not forget to take care of yourself. After all, your child needs a strong support system.

The next step is to take action. Now that you have all the information you need, start applying it and help your child overcome their anxiety. The sooner you begin, the easier it will be to solve their problems. Since young minds are unaware of how to handle and deal with unfavorable situations, you have to step in and alleviate the symptoms as their guardian.

Finally, if you found the book useful and wish other parents to gain insights on treating their child's anxiety, leave a review for this book to reach as many parents as possible.

REFERENCES

6 hidden signs of teen anxiety. (n.d.). Retrieved from Psycom.net website:
https://www.psycom.net/hidden-signs-teen-anxiety/

6 things you should never say to teens with anxiety disorders. (2016, October 5). Retrieved from Discoverymood.comwebsite:
https://discoverymood.com/blog/6-things-never-say-teensanxiety-disorders/

10 things never to say to your anxious child. (n.d.). Retrieved from Psycom.net website:
https://www.psycom.net/childanxiety-things-never-to-say

Amy Morin, L. (n.d.). How to help a shy teen build selfconfidence. Retrieved from Verywellfamily.com website:
https://www.verywellfamily.com/how-to-help-a-shy-teenbuild-self-confidence-2611009

Ankrom, S., MS, & LCPC. (n.d.). The difference between fear and anxiety. Retrieved from Verywellmind.com website:
https://www.verywellmind.com/fear-and-anxiety-differencesand-similarities-2584399

Anxiety in teens - how to help a teenager deal with anxiety - hey Sigmund. (2016, October 21). Retrieved from Heysigmund.com website:

https://www.heysigmund.com/anxiety-in-teens/
Anxiety in Teens is Rising: What's Going On? (n.d.). Retrieved from Healthychildren.org website: https://www.healthychildren.org/English/healthissues/conditions/emotional-problems/Pages/AnxietyDisorders.aspx

Can gastric disorders contribute to Anxiety and Depression?(n.d.). Retrieved from Mentalhelp.net website: https://www.mentalhelp.net/blogs/can-gastric-disorderscontribute-to-anxiety-and-depression/

Cho, J. (2016, June 1). 13 things about social anxiety disorder you may not have known. Forbes Magazine. Retrieved from https://www.forbes.com/sites/jeenacho/2016/06/01/13-thingsabout-social-anxiety-disorder-you-may-not-have-known/

Helping your anxious child or teen. (n.d.). Retrieved from Heretohelp.bc.ca website: https://www.heretohelp.bc.ca/infosheet/helping-your-anxiouschild-or-teen

Holland, K. (2018, September 19). Anxiety: Causes, symptoms, treatment, and more. Retrieved from Healthline.com website: https://www.healthline.com/health/anxiety

Managing and treating anxiety. (n.d.). Retrieved from Gov.au website:

https://www.betterhealth.vic.gov.au/health/condi tionsandtreat ments/anxiety-treatment-options

Matheis, L. (n.d.). The do's and don'ts of parenting an anxious
teen. Psychology Today. Retrieved from https://www.psychologytoday.com/blog/special matters/201904/the-dos-and-don-ts-parenting-anxious-teen

Meyerowitz, A. (2018, June 6). 13 physical symptoms you didn't know were caused by anxiety. Retrieved from Redonline.co.uk website: https://www.redonline.co.uk/healthself/self/a528 103/13-physical-symptoms-you-didnt-knowwere-caused-by-anxiety/

Mindfulness – is it for you? (n.d.). Retrieved from Reachout.com website: https://au.reachout.com/articles/mindfulness-is-it-foryou

Morgan, K. (n.d.). How anxiety affects your focus. BBC. Retrieved from https://www.bbc.com/worklife/article/20200611 how-anxiety-affects-your-focus

Northwestern Medicine. (n.d.). The impact of unspoken peer pressure. Retrieved from Www.nm.org website: https://www.nm.org/healthbeat/healthy-tips/emotionalhealth/unspoken-peer-pressure

O'Grady, S. J. (2018, August 30). Social anxiety disorder: When fear leads to isolation. Retrieved from Webmd.com website: https://blogs.webmd.com/mental-health/20180830/socialanxiety-disorder-when-fear-leads-to-isolation

ReachOut Australia. (2020, October 14). What is anxiety? Retrieved from Reachout.com website: https://au.reachout.com/articles/what-is-anxiety

Spector, N. (2019, May 20). A mental health check-in: 14 questions to ask your child. Retrieved from NBC News website: https://www.nbcnews.com/better/lifestyle/mental-healthcheck-14-questions-ask-your-child-ncna1006936

Teen depression and anxiety: What parents can do to help. (2018, October 13). Retrieved from Lynnlyons.com website: https://www.lynnlyons.com/teen-depression-anxiety/

Wright, L. W. (2019, September 17). Signs of anxiety in tweens and teens. Retrieved from Understood.org website: https://www.understood.org/en/friends-feelings/managingfeelings/stress-anxiety/signs-your-teen-or-tween-is-strugglingwith-anxiety

(N.d.-a). Retrieved from Adaa.org website: https://adaa.org/understanding-anxiety

(N.d.-b). Retrieved from Apa.org website: https://www.apa.org/monitor/2013/07-08/dull-moment

ways to deal with anxiety. (n.d.). Retrieved from Kidshealth.org website: https://kidshealth.org/en/teens/anxiety-tips.html

hidden signs of teen anxiety. (n.d.). Retrieved from Psycom.net website: https://www.psycom.net/hidden-signs-teen-anxiety/

Anxiety in teenagers. (2020, July 17). Retrieved from Net.au website: https://raisingchildren.net.au/pre-teens/mental-healthphysical-health/stress-anxiety-depression/anxiety

Anxiety medications for teens: Treatment options for your child. (n.d.). Retrieved from Psycom.net website: https://www.psycom.net/anxiety-medications-teenagers

Cherney, K. (2014, September 24). Effects of anxiety on the body. Retrieved from Healthline.com website: https://www.healthline.com/health/anxiety/effects-on-body

Common Causes of Anxiety in Teens and Young Adults. (2020, May 26). Retrieved from Paradigmtreatment.com website:

https://paradigmtreatment.com/anxiety-teens-youngadults/common-causes/

Villiers, D. (2020, April 24). Is my child's anxiety "normal"? Retrieved from Anxietyinstitute.com website:
https://anxietyinstitute.com/is-my-childs-anxiety-normal/

Anxiety in teenagers. (2020, July 17). Raising Children Network.
https://raisingchildren.net.au/preteens/mentalhealthphysicalhealth/stressanxietydepression/anxiety#:%7E:text=If%20your%20teenage%20child%20is,giving%20a%20presentation%20in%20class.

Banes, K. (2016, April 1). 6 ways good parents contribute to their child's anxiety. Washington Post.
https://www.washingtonpost.com/news/parenting/wp/2016/0 4/01/6-ways-good-parents-contribute-to-their-childs-anxiety/

Doyle, K. (2013, December 13). Parent behaviors linked to kids' anxiety, depression. U.S.
https://www.reuters.com/article/usparent-kids-anxiety-depression-idUSBRE9BC0VR20131213

Li, P. (2021, March 25). Controlling Parents – The Signs And Why They Are Harmful. Parenting For Brain.
https://www.parentingforbrain.com/controlling-parents/

Lindberg, S. L. (2020, September 25). Bad Parenting: Signs, Effects, and How to Change It. Healthline. https://www.healthline.com/health/parenting/badparenting#signs

Walton, A. G. (2012, August 3). How Parents' Stress Can Hurt A Child, From The Inside Out. Forbes. https://www.forbes.com/sites/alicegwalton/2012/07/25/howparents-stress-can-hurt-a-child-from-the-insideout/?sh=2d87260f6b38

Building a Crisis Kit. (2020, September 28). The Recovery Village Drug and Alcohol Rehab. https://www.therecoveryvillage.com/mentalhealth/related/crisis-kits/

Halloran, J. (2021, January 9). Coping Skill Spotlight: 5 4 3 2 1 Grounding Technique. Coping Skills forKids. https://copingskillsforkids.com/blog/2016/4/27/coping-skillspotlight-5-4-3-2-1-grounding-technique

Helping someone with anxiety and panic attacks. (n.d.). Mind. https://www.mind.org.uk/information-support/types-ofmental-health-problems/anxiety-and-panic-attacks/for-friendsand-family/

How to Help Someone with Anxiety. (n.d.). Johns Hopkins Medicine.

https://www.hopkinsmedicine.org/health/treatme
nttests-and-therapies/how-to-help-someone-with-
anxiety

Reframe Anxiety Thoughts. (n.d.). Yahoo.
https://www.yahoo.com/lifestyle/reframe-
anxiety-thoughtsnow-using-111522096.html

Why worrying isn't always a bad thing. (2013,
January 13). Independent.
https://www.independent.ie/regionals/herald/life
style/healthbeauty/why-worrying-isnt-always-a-bad-
thing-27980020.html

Young, K. (2020, August 7). Anxiety in Teens –
How to Help a Teenager Deal With Anxiety. Hey
Sigmund.
https://www.heysigmund.com/anxiety-in-teens/

Schab, L., 2008. The anxiety workbook for teens.
Oakland, CA: Instant Help Books.

Chambala, A. (2008). Anxiety and Art Therapy:
Treatment in the Public Eye. Art Therapy, 25(4), 187-
189. Ankrom, S. (2021). Deep Breathing Exercises to
Reduce Anxiety. Retrieved from
https://www.verywellmind.com/abdominalbreathi
ng-2584115

Schab, L. (2008). Anxiety Workbook for Teens.
[Place of publication not identified]: New Harbinger
Publications.

Vick, R. (1999). Utilizing Prestructured Art
Elements in Brief

Group Art Therapy with Adolescents. Art Therapy, 16(2), 68-77.

Amy Morin, L. (n.d.). 15 Self-Care Strategies for Parents. Retrieved from Verywellfamily.com website: https://www.verywellfamily.com/self-care-for-parents4178010

Burton, N. (2020, November 2). Self-care strategies for parents when you have no time for yourself. Retrieved from Healthline.com website: https://www.healthline.com/health/parenting/self-carestrategies-for-parents-no-time

Gene Beresin, Executive Director, & Braaten, E. (2020, January 8). 10 self-care tips for parents. Retrieved from Mghclaycenter.org website: https://www.mghclaycenter.org/parentingconcerns/10-self-care-tips-for-parents/

Parents passing anxiety to children. (2016, February 23). Retrieved from Childmind.org website: https://childmind.org/article/how-to-avoid-passing-anxietyon-to-your-kids/

Self-care and support for parents and caregivers of young children (14). (n.d.). Retrieved from Gov.au website: https://www.betterhealth.vic.gov.au/health/HealthyLiving/selfcare-support-for-parents-caregiver-14

THE
END

Made in the USA
Middletown, DE
19 September 2022